Politics in the Human Interest

Politics in the Human Interest

Applying Sociology in the Real World

William Du Bois and R. Dean Wright

LEXINGTON BOOKS

A division of
ROWMAN & LITTLEFIELD PUBLISHERS, INC.
Lanham • Boulder • New York • Toronto • Plymouth, UK

LEXINGTON BOOKS

A division of Rowman & Littlefield Publishers, Inc.
A wholly owned subsidiary of The Rowman & Littlefield Publishing Group, Inc.
4501 Forbes Boulevard, Suite 200
Lanham, MD 20706

Estover Road
Plymouth PL6 7PY
United Kingdom

British Library Cataloguing in Publication Information Available

Library of Congress Cataloging-in-Publication Data

Du Bois, William D. (William David)
  Politics in the human interest : applying sociology in the real world / William Du Bois
and R. Dean Wright.
     p. cm.
  ISBN-13: 978-0-7391-1770-5 (cloth : alk. paper)
  ISBN-10: 0-7391-1770-X (cloth : alk. paper)
  ISBN-13: 978-0-7391-1771-2 (pbk. : alk. paper)
  ISBN-10: 0-7391-1771-8 (pbk. : alk. paper)
  1. Applied sociology. 2. Social change. 3. Social problems. I. Wright, R. Dean. II.
Title.
  HN29.5.D85 2007
  303.4—dc22   2007002445

Printed in the United States of America

⊖™ The paper used in this publication meets the minimum requirements of American
National Standard for Information Sciences—Permanence of Paper for Printed Library
Materials, ANSI/NISO Z39.48–1992.

Table of Contents

INTRODUCTION

Applying Sociology in the Real World

The purpose of knowledge is to promote the art of living.
—philosopher Alfred Whitehead

Sociology by its very nature is political. Our calling is to make a better world. The founders of the discipline thought sociology would gather knowledge about human behavior and then apply that knowledge to improve society. It's as political an agenda as you can get. Yet most sociologists today are afraid to openly profess sociology. They shy from controversy. They disguise values and accept the premise that academic professionals should keep values out of their work. Academic sociology is lost in this sea of relativism.
Yet the early sociologists saw social progress and human betterment as the very goals of social science. As they knew, value relativism disappears once we ground the enterprise in human needs. Pulitzer prize winning sociologist Ernest Becker (1968: 45) summarizes: "if science is centered on man and subserves him, and if progress is its goal, then, logically, when we find out the social causes of human unhappiness, we will have an automatic directive to an agreed solution."
The purpose of our knowledge is to promote human well-being. Our values are the human agenda. Sociology grew up with the promise that it would provide the basis for a new politics—a politics in the human interest. Those who say we should keep our values out of our work don't understand sociology. The whole point of the discipline is to create a political agenda that is in the human interest. The ancient Greek philosophers had dreamed of a Science of Community (a science of the "polis" as they put it). Aristotle had dreamed of a Science of Happiness. We have the knowledge to implement it today.
August Comte, who is normally considered the founder of sociology, thought sociologists should sit at the right hand of the leader of government riding shotgun so to speak—watching the map, advising which way to turn to reach a destination and alerting the driver if we are headed in the wrong direction. Thomas Jefferson had dreamed of a National Academy. He felt that knowledge,

human progress, and democracy go together. Lester Ward who coined the name "Applied Sociology" pictured an applied national academy in Washington, D.C. to train lawmakers how to create the good society. It may have been the original idea for a think tank.

In the late nineteenth century when American sociology was born, people were concerned with what was then called "the social problem." What problems can be solved through collective action by changing the conditions in which people live? However, the conservatives of Lester Ward's day thought it was folly to hope for human betterment. They argued that evil is intrinsic to human nature and pointed to the persistence of social problems as proof. In their view, to think social problems could be remedied or that we could create a good society that improved upon human behavior was simply a delusion. The best society could hope for was to keep problems at bay. According to his biographer, Ward thought the reason we haven't made much social progress making a better world

> is not found in evil human nature, but in the lack of applied social science, and the stubborn resistance of even so-called moral elements in society to any basic improvements in the condition of the mass. . . . Instead of preaching morality in the midst of an immoral social system of dog eat dog, . . . Ward argues for an entirely new concept of ethics based upon an intelligent, planned social order in which the principle of 'every man for himself' . . . will not exist. (Chugerman, 1939: pp. 547–549)

As we will see, much of sociology and psychology has shown what religion has argued all along—that selfishness is not practical. Self and community are intricately interwoven. We need an enlightened self interest that transcends narrow selfishness.

In the last 150 years of social science, we have learned a great deal about the causes of social problems and how to create a better society in which people thrive. It should be a simple lesson. Some social conditions bring out the best in people. Others bring out their worst. Human systems that don't meet human needs have increased social problems. And trying to keep the lid on with brute force is expensive, wasteful of human life, dangerous—and ultimately ineffective.

We have been told that we should be objective. But what if after having studied a body of knowledge, we reach some conclusions? And what if those conclusions fly in the face of the current political agenda? It is not scholarly to refrain from educating the public about what we've learned.

Alfred McClung Lee who coined the words "humanistic sociology" thought there were two key problems. One is how to build a better society. The other is the question of "knowledge for whom?" Whom does sociology serve?

Most think tanks today are a far cry from what Lester Ward imagined. They are designed to fit a predetermined agenda—to serve the clients' special interests not the human interest. And yet we could build a humanistic sociology— one that serves the human interest. We could create a better society.

Lester Ward's vision of a think tank to teach lawmakers what's been learned about human behavior and how to make the good society still makes sense. His analysis and recommendation are as relevant today as when they were conceived in the 1870s: "The rich simply grow richer, and the poor, poorer, and the number of people who have nothing but vanished hopes increases. The only rational solution to this paradox, Ward repeats, is found in applied sociology . . . [b]y giving more attention to the problem of happiness and less to that of amassing wealth" (Chugerman, 1939: pp. 547–549).

Together, we can build a better society. Thomas Kunen in his book *The Structure of Scientific Revolutions* showed that scientific laws are agreements of those who have studied a body of knowledge. Social science leads to some conclusions.

Economist Kenneth Boulding once said the question for the social sciences is simply "what is better and how do we get there?" Sociologists have learned quite a bit about the answer.

SECTION I

POLITICS IN THE HUMAN INTEREST

Chapter 1:

The Politics of Sociology

Sociology was born at a time that people thought knowledge could be used to make a better world. However today, the sociological perspective is in danger of being erased. We're back to the founding arguments of the discipline. Is there even such a thing as society? Or can everything be explained in terms of individuals? Back in the 1980s, Conservative former British Prime Minister Margaret Thatcher voiced this popular psychological reductionism blatantly: "there is no society, there are only individuals and families."

Such a failure to see the social means we don't think in terms of social solutions. We don't see that people in similar situations often have common needs. We don't ask, what kinds of social resources would be helpful to individuals in such situations? Two hundred years ago people didn't understand that building public sewers and public sanitation were essential for everybody's health. The great plagues swept across Europe. People thought diseases were a product of moral failings. Only after we realized the connections were we able to build the kind of resources necessary to prevent diseases from happening.

Politicians today retreat to primitive versions of economics and political science that were popular before the birth of sociology, anthropology and psychology painted a more complex picture. When things go wrong, most today blame only the individual. They demand people try harder and make better rational choices. When that doesn't work, they call out the troops or cops to force people to behave.

In the late nineteenth century when American sociology was born, people were concerned with what was then called "the social problem." What problems can be solved through collective action by changing the conditions in which people live? Pick up any social problems book and you'll find a "social problem" defined as something that can be solved by collective action. Put that way, most people today don't believe in social problems anymore. Everything's just a personal problem. If you're not making it, it's your own fault.

Albion Small chaired the first American sociology department which was at the University of Chicago. He said, his entire life's work was to overcome what he called "the individualistic superstition." About the same time, Emile Durkheim cautioned that if someone gives you an individual explanation of a social phenomena, you can be pretty sure that it is wrong.[1] Social problems are not simply the product of bad individuals and poor personal choices. We have a great deal of convincing evidence that there are numerous social factors. The perspective that we can just untax the rich, deregulate corporations and trust social problems to take care of themselves is ignorant of what's been learned about human behavior.

However, most social scientists are too chicken to say that. We politely pander to all sides for fear of offending. This is nonsense. It's like trying to teach auto repair to a group of faith healers who think they're just not concentrating hard enough when they fail to visualize their car's problems gone. We are going to have to teach them a different method if we want that car to be driving down the road anytime soon. Similarly, we are never going to remedy social problems by ignoring root social causes and just insisting individuals try harder. Individual problems are not the result of moral failings as conservatives of the late nineteenth century and the early twenty first century maintain. It's the system that has to change. But the most sacred conservative covenant is "hands off the system." And those profiting off "the way things are" sure don't want us checking underneath the hood. But we are going to have to if we're going to fix the problems.

The Sociological Imagination

The conscious creation of human systems goes by the name of politics.

—Arthur Warmoth, former president, *Association for Humanistic Psychology*

Applied sociology is politics. We can invent social resources individuals can use to address personal troubles. C. Wright Mills would later call this the *sociological imagination*: the ability to see the interrelation between personal troubles and social problems Lester Ward knew it. August Comte dreamed of it. Jane Addams articulated it 100 years ago:

> a man of high moral culture [is] one who thinks of himself, not as an isolated individual, but as a part in a social organism. Upon this foundation it ought not to be difficult to build a structure for civic virtue. It is only necessary to make it clear to the voter that his individual needs are common needs, that is, public needs, and that they can only be legitimately supplied for him when they are supplied for all. (Addams, 1902: 117)

The Sociological Imagination is as political an agenda as you can get. It is translating personal problems into social issues. It is asking, what social resources could we invent to help individuals in their struggles? Many say, "nah, we can't do that" or more expressly, "we don't want to pay for that." They ignore most good social science because it implies the need to fund social solutions.

The New Deal was probably the first time we saw social problems as not individual but social and approached solutions with social answers (WPA, CCC camps, work projects, social security, etc., etc.). Franklin Roosevelt realized living conditions were related to crime. Posters were even produced to educate the public that eliminating slum conditions was a way to reduce crime. C. Wright Mills knew that individual troubles could often be addressed more effectively by creating social resources. Lyndon Johnson's Great Society came out of a vast amount of sociological research. Politicians were listening to sociologists. They knew poverty was connected to crime. The war on poverty was designed to get to the roots of crime. But most politicians today have declared war only on individual criminals and abandoned attention to social factors.

Society Done It: Where the Liberals Went Wrong (Part 1)

In the 1960s, a naive version of sociology emerged in the mind of the public: Society done it. The poor criminal is just a victim of society. Criminals should be pitied. They have a social disease. This simplistic pop sociology rightly fell into disfavor with the public. It is the "oversocialized" conception of society Dennis Wrong had warned about—seeing individuals as only products of social forces and having no free will. The public rightly demanded an inclusion of individual responsibility.

Of course, individuals are responsible for their actions. But if we as a society know the social causes of social problems and refuse to do anything about them, aren't we also responsible? To blame only the individual ignores the fact that although individuals come and go, the environment grows a new crop of people with the same social problems year after year. We need to look at both individual and societal responsibility. Just because the individual is responsible does not mean that society should get off the hook, or vica versa. Victim Offender Reconciliation Program founder Howard Zehr reminds that saying individuals are responsible for crime does not mean that there are not also social dimensions of responsibility.

The sociological perspective is not that individuals are not responsible for their actions but that different environments make some behaviors more likely and others less probable. Healthy choices are only likely to take place in the context of viable alternatives. The social resources available when you act influence what is going to happen. We can change the odds by seeding social resources into the environment that help individuals in their struggles. Or we can just abandon individuals to their own devices.

Step right up and place your bets. Where do you want to put your money? Do you believe we come together and invent social solutions? Or do you want to fund tax cuts for the rich and trust the market to take care of all problems? And if that doesn't work, we can always spend a fortune on prisons and the military to make people behave. It's your money. What makes sense to you?

What Comes After the New Deal—New Ideas or Old Ideas?

When the New Deal coalition of northern liberals and southern populists fell apart in the late 1970s, we had a choice. We either could admit that we were in new territory and needed new ideas, or we could go back and check out the shadow side of critics who had always followed after the New Deal. It seemed less frightening to return to the past than venture into unfamiliar, uncharted waters. [2] Ronald Reagan was the perfect spokesperson for a retreat into the safe and comfortable past. The solution is free markets. Keep the government out of it. There is no need for social planning. The social system will take care of itself. Rather than mend old programs or invent new ones, we were told to abandon the very idea of social solutions and trust the wisdom of the market.

Today's conservatives advocate much the same things as those 100 years ago. We still haven't taken the step into new territory. They say there is no need for government to protect us from the will of vast corporations. We should deregulate industry. We can trust the private sector to take care of public needs. As much as Bush and Cheney want to package themselves as a "new kind of Republican," it is really a return to the policies of Calvin Coolidge and Herbert Hoover. Only this time, it's gone global.

Many of the battles that were fought out 100 years ago in the United States are now being staged on a world wide scale. And ironically, it is the same industries that were involved then: big oil companies, banking, and the garment industry.

In 1984, Gary Hart ran in the presidential primary on the platform that we needed new ideas. He was right. Unfortunately, he himself didn't have any. Sociology ought to be at the vanguard offering new solutions. But we have been relegated to the sidelines. Today's applied sociologists do market research, focus groups, and public opinion polling. Meanwhile, conservatives have launched a war to invalidate the very idea of social solutions.

Imaginative social programs are not even being discussed because conservatives have been so successful at promoting their agenda of blaming the individual for social problems. The voice supporting social change in order to make the world a better place for everyone has all but been silenced. The conservative agenda which supports a fundamental belief in the individual has so captured the American value system that there is literally no room left for an alternative point of view. Along with the acceptance of individualism as a core value trails accompanying ideas espousing personal control, hard work, success, materialism, and rationality.

Traditionally there were "liberals" who challenged and questioned the validity of this point of view, arguing that society was built on relationships among people. However, liberals have retreated from the public debate. We hear only the proposed solutions of conservatives which are thinly disguised ways to deplete social programs and turn public monies and resources over to the private sector. In an era of tax cut fever, politicians are reluctant to even think about exploring new social solutions.

Notes

1. "Consequently, every time that a social phenomenon is directly explained by psychological phenomenon, we may be sure that the explanation is false." Emile Durkheim, *Rules of Sociological Method*. The Free Press, New York: [1895] 1964, p. 104.

2. This stunning observation is from a conversation with Art Warmoth.

Chapter 2:

Sociology and Social Change

A funny thing happened on the way to a science of human behavior. The early sociologists thought they would discover the causes of social problems and policy makers would gobble up their knowledge and create a better world. They had no idea that "the powers that be" would actively seek to suppress and distort their knowledge.

Reflecting on society eventually leads to conclusions about the causes of social problems and effective remedies. But in a world where the turf has already been divided up, solutions are likely to step on toes those profiting off the way things are. Even if it would benefit everyone in the long run, their knee jerk reaction is to leave things alone. Ernest Becker showed in *The Lost Science of Man* that the dilemmas Albion Small faced in creating the first sociology department in the United States at the University of Chicago are contemporary. They are the very struggles we face today.

> a mature social science would have to be socially experimental . . . . a mature social science would have to be socially critical, critical of the very institutions and accepted habits that society thinks it needs in order to sustain its very life. (1971: 42)

What Becker calls the "Paradox of Sociology" is that due of its very nature, sociology is a discipline destined to bite the hand that feeds it. Complicating the matter is the fact that sociologists are beholden to "the powers that be" both for funding and to disseminate their findings. It is the predicament of both educators and news reporters. The emperor may wish to shoot the messenger rather than hear the message. We are reminded of the Iowa legislator who several years ago who tried to get an Iowa State University professor fired because she'd said people should eat more white meat and less red meat. After all, as the legislator said, Iowa is a beef producing state and a state employee should not be saying that.

Many have said sociology has never had a breakthrough of public recognition. It has never had its Freud or Einstein. It's not that sociologists haven't produced impressive results. We know a great deal about the causes social problems and how to solve them. It is just that it is not what the powers that be want to hear.

It reminds of the president of the large organization who convenes a committee to fish until they come up with the conclusions he has already decided upon. However, knowledge doesn't work that way. And this is precisely the problems conservatives have with academics. We often dispute their foregone conclusions.

Conservatives are upset that academia is liberal. They consider that to be bias and want to make sure the conservative viewpoint is adequately represented. But if you study social problems, you can't know what is going on and still embrace recommendations that focus only on the individual. A person educated in sociology isn't likely to be an ultra right wing conservative any more than a brain surgeon is likely to be a Christian Scientist.

In the 1960s, sociology did briefly become public knowledge but it was attacked as ideology and has since been successfully marginalized by public relations firms in a propaganda war. Scientists in all fields were naive. They never dreamed slick public relations firms would distort their findings trying to establish a paper trail in court to muddy the water about substances and pollution causing cancer, deny the existence of global warming caused by fossil fuels, or refuse to acknowledge that poverty causes crime.

The Best Sociology Is Often Mistaken for Ideology

"Some of the best social science is still considered ideology and opinion," wrote Ernest Becker (1971: 60).

In the late 1960s, Attorney General Ramsey Clark noted in his book *Crime in America* that if you take a map and circle the areas with the worst housing, worst poverty, highest unemployment, and the least services you would have circled all the areas with the highest crime rates. He argued that we should do something about the environments that produce crime rather than just focusing on the individual criminals. But we as a society have retreated from such conclusions. Conservatives no doubt would see this as old fashioned liberal thinking—an outdated political ideology that we should have given up years ago. To conclude that large disparities in income is a major cause of crime is the ultimate heresy to the agenda of rich conservatives. Conservatives would hope we have "outgrown" such "New Deal" ideas.

When you can compare a map of nuclear radiation across the world with a map of cancer rates, you find a remarkable similarity. You can compare a list of high school classmates who died before they were sixty with a list of those who smoked all those years and also find considerable consistency. That does not mean you are ideologically biased against nuclear plants and the tobacco industry. Similarly, noticing that environments with high crime rates share certain characteristics is not ideology—it is good science. Creating meaningful jobs, job training and opportunities for a better life reduce crime rates. However, that is viewed as liberal ideology rather than the solid social science it is.

Conservatives would like to deny such conclusions for purely ideological reasons—it does not fit their pre-formed conclusions. It also does not fit their pocketbooks. If the root causes of social problems are social causes, we as a society are going to have to invest in social resources if we are going to remedy social ills.

Max Weber wrote:

The primary task of a useful teacher is to teach his students to recognize 'inconvenient' facts—I mean facts that are inconvenient for their party opinions. And for every party opinion there are facts that are extremely inconvenient, for my own opinion no less than for others (Weber, 1918).

Weber felt no amount of "scientific pleading" was likely to get someone to recognize such "inconvenient facts." He said that the willingness to admit the existence of inconvenient facts that fly in the face of one's political interests might even be called a "moral achievement."

There are conclusions which emerge from thinking sociologically. However, for those whose chief agenda the past twenty years has been lowering taxes for the richest Americans, it is so much easier to believe bad individuals are the causes of social problems and blame them. The sociological perspective itself is inconvenient information for the ultra conservative agenda. If social problems are actually caused by social factors, then we as a society are going to have to fund viable social solutions to have success. That is indeed inconvenient information for the richest Americans whose taxes have been cut in half from what they had been for the fifty years from the 1930 to 1980. We must realize that ultra conservatives launched a war on sociological explanations for this explicit reason—they do not want to have to fund social programs.

A key bit of sociological knowledge—it is not ideology but fact—is that nations with a higher distances between the rich and the poor have higher crime and more social problems. It is the perfect example of an "inconvenient fact" that flies in the face of the conservative ideology. We can simply not have a world where the rich get richer and the poor cannot meet their basic needs, without paying the consequences in an array of social problems.

Bizarrely, explanations which see the consequences of the social environment are termed ideology while explanations which blindly cling to the individual as the sole cause are termed common sense.

The War on Knowledge: Manipulating Science and the Media

Progressive think tanks feel an honest presentation on what we know about social problems leads inevitably to progressive recommendations for social policy. They feel all that is necessary is for them to present their data and research.

Most academics and liberals don't get it. Conservatives have no intention of having an honest discussion. They hire public relations firms and fund think tanks to sell their agenda. Like cops planting evidence on someone they already "know" is guilty, they are out to win at all costs. As Trudy Lieberman (2000: 38) in *Slanting the Story* says, whereas liberal think tanks

embrace the academy not to influence government programs but to produce a neutral scientific evaluation of a particular activity. Conservative groups have the opposite goal. . . . the right wing economic elite pour money into these so-called think tanks to pretend that independent research verifies their world view.

The right wing has learned to use social science as a tool of spin doctoring and have been very successful at managing the media. The ideology of objectivity makes journalists and social scientists particularly easy prey for manipulation. When one side tries to present an accurate picture and the other side is trying to fool the public, public education is in trouble as journalists try to present a balanced view by splitting the difference. Like a sincere person haggling over the price with a crooked used car dealer, when you split the difference down the middle between honesty and lies, you get a distorted picture of the bottom line.

"Education" means literally "to lead forth." Earlier, we noted the problem of the university leading in new directions when it is dependent upon outside "powers that be" for funding. Think tanks collapse this line completely. They are little more than propaganda mills set up to benefit their clients' interests. The Cato Institute, American Enterprise Institute and Heritage Foundation are not going to recommend massive government spending on social programs no matter what their "research" concludes. Indeed, such runs counter to their mission statements.[1]

The right wing has learned to use social science as a tool of spin doctoring. They are little more than professional liars but they have become very good at it. They have been aided and abetted by a value free social science that straddles all issues, engages in academic hair splitting, embraces obscure philosophical technicalities and refuses to call a spade a spade.

If you can get expert testimony to confirm your worldview, you can make a good case in court or with public opinion. At the very least you can claim, "well, the experts disagree." Many are not aware that there is a deep seeded campaign to fill research journals with the "proper" perspectives. The tobacco industry has turned this into an art form funding their own journals. They even fund conferences with respectable scientists and then publish the proceedings planting an article or two with their own perspective which can be later cited in other journals (or in court). It is all a high stakes propaganda campaign. *Consumer Reports* (January 1995, pp. 27–33) did a nice job several years ago detailing the tobacco folks' efforts to create a paper trail in regards to second hand smoke.

In the social sciences, data is often associational rather than absolute mechanical cause and effect. Some may argue that we can't therefore say poverty causes crime. This is the same argument that the tobacco companies use. Tobacco lobbyists argue you cannot say smoking causes cancer because we have only correlational data. Some people smoke and never get lung cancer. Some people live in horrible neighborhoods and don't turn to crime. We are dealing in probabilities. Of course, there are exceptions. However, smoking cigarettes increases the odds of getting cancer. You can say the same thing about the relationship between most environmental pollution and diseases. We have only correlational data. But esoteric arguments aside, most of us would say smoking causes cancer.

We can come to reasonable conclusions that have clear implications for social policy just as the data on smoking and lung cancer can influence our decision to quit smoking. Extreme poverty increases the likelihood of a variety of social ills including crime, alcohol, and drugs. That is *not a value judgment.*

Sociology concludes individuals are more likely to turn to crime in some circumstances than others.

Someone has to educate the public to see the world sociologically. The sociological perspective itself is seldom promoted in the media. The public hears it only on rare occasions whereas they are subject to the constant drone of a contrived effort to promote a conservative perspective which is intensely anti-sociological. On the other hand, efforts to promote the sociological perspective have no financial backers, a total disarray of unified action, and an ineptitude of strategies.

However, the main reason sociologists cannot effectively confront their conservative naysayers is because of an unresolved epistemological dilemma. Foundations that support progressive causes actually have several times more money than conservative foundations. However, they don't see it as an ideological battle whereas the conservatives know full well that it is.

> If progressive organizations are to reclaim ground in the ideological war, they must rethink what they stand for, be brave enough to tell the public, and sell their ideas more forcefully (Lieberman, 2000: 164).

The Liberal Dilemma—Where Liberals Went Wrong (Part 2)

Liberals and progressive foundations feel ideology is tainted. Sociologists are reluctant to move beyond a value free approach. Although, many have discarded the scientific notion of finding the truth, they still maintain strict allegiance to the ideology of being value free and non-partisan.

Is everything just a matter of opinion? Do we know anything as sociologists? If our students take an Introduction to Sociology class and then still vote for Rush Limbaugh and Bill O'Reilly, have we taught them sociology? Is it just a matter of values to think poverty occurs because people are lazy? Or that crime occurs because people are bad? If someone completed a class in biology and still came away thinking the reason many old people lose their teeth is because of the tooth fairy—or that the flu is caused by cooties, would we consider that just a matter of opinion?

It is understandable why liberals are cautious. When we try to make the Good, we are in dangerous territory. One person's utopia often is another person's worst nightmare. History is full of examples of true believers who made the world much worse in their attempts to make it better. Ernest Becker in *Escape from Evil* claims most of the evil in the world actually originates from efforts to stamp out evil. But this does not mean all efforts to make the good are misguided and doomed to make things worse. The liberal dilemma is that having seen the abuses that have historically occurred when one pursues values as social policy, they may stay forever at the crossroads afraid to take a step in any direction.

The conservatives are right that people need values. We need a frame of reference to prioritize and guide our actions. The question is: which values?

It is a conversation liberals would just as soon not have. But while they sit it out, they give the world to the conservatives and fundamentalists who have no reservations about offering their visions. In a world hungry for meaning, many have responded. The left is not offering an alternative vision of the Good Society.

To many conservatives, their perspective is truth and all else is spin. The ultra conservative Fox News Network labels their biased perspective as "The No Spin Zone." Pat Buchanan who penned Agnew's famous speech attacking the media, sees his worldview as reality. Anything else is media bias.

On the other hand, liberals understand that all truth is from a perspective. What you see depends upon your values—what is important, where you look, and how. It is all much like Einstein's theory of relativity. So how should we look? What matters?

Cultural relativity means taking off your values long enough to see, understanding other's behavior in their terms. It doesn't mean not to have values. Human beings need values to live.

When we talk of bias in reporting, what we really mean is someone who refuses to look except from their own perspective. The value of objectivity does not mean not having values, but in taking off your values long enough to see. The grain of truth in objectivity that is worth keeping is the commitment not to falsify what we see. The essential component is honesty. Spin violates all that. Spin doctors have no intention of such honesty.

To share to global village, we can no longer go to our own private corners of the universe. This is not like some old episode of *Star Trek* where we let each worldview survive on its own planet. We share one world and our perspectives collide. We need a larger meta-conversation about values. On what can we agree? An answer of "nothing" relegates the conversation to the fundamentalists who are very sure of what they would make. Fundamentalists seeking the extermination of other perspectives in a Final Solution are actively fighting for control of the earth. In an age of nuclear, chemical and biological weapons such perspectives are a threat to the survival of the human race whether the fundamentalists call themselves Christians, Muslims, Hindus or Jews. Unless we as human beings come together and reach a shared agreement about values, we are perpetually going to be at war. We must come together as humans with a more sane synthesis.

Beyond Relativism and Spin

It's hard to make that effort to think how the other person feels. But that's really what a moral life is, an ethical life is. It's trying to take in some of the reality of what other people feel or how they see things from their point of view. Which doesn't mean that everybody has their own opinion. I'm not a relativist either. And I don't think every belief is worthy of respect.

—Susan Sontag on *Now with Bill Moyers*, April 4, 2003

Liberals believe in listening to others and respecting their truths. They would teach tolerance and diversity. But what do you do about the bully or the batterer? They have no intention of playing fair.

Peacemaking criminologist Hal Pepinsky defines violence as refusing to take others into account or to alter one's course. He says the opposite of violence is democracy. Democracy is about dialog. We learn to take each other into account. It is about hearing and responding to others' needs.

One view that should not be respected is those who are lying to us—who purposely are trying to distort and manipulate us. This, you will notice, is the very definition of modern public relations and much of what goes by the name of politics.

A company that knows its products are harmful but sets out to deceive the public is not worthy of respect. Lawyers battling in court to win at all costs are not interested in honest dialogue or the truth coming to the top. Public relations consultants paid to make clients look good even though they are doing despicable things are not interested in a fair presentation. For academics to treat the substance of such debates as legitimate makes us ripe for manipulation.

Science was founded on the idea that rational discourse would lead to agreements. Our legal system assumes the truth will naturally surface from an adversarial contest. But that is not always true. Power intervenes and distorts perception. The new crew of lawyers, spin doctors, media con artists, and public relations consultants turn rationality into a weapon. Some will tell any lie to get their way. For them, the end justifies the means. Journalists assume merely reciting the spin of both sides will provide an objective, "non-biased" presentation of the news. But that is far from true. The public (and journalists) get spun from side to side. In our postmodern age, most people have become dizzy and don't know what to think. They are lost in the postmodern dilemma where everything is relative and all is spin.

The way out of the whole postmodern dilemma is a commitment to honesty. We must be honest about what we see and what we need. Fromm notes that respect is to see someone (or something) as what he or she (or it) is. Respect means to not falsify things. The core worth keeping in the idea of "objectivity" is to be honest about what we see.

> objectivity is not, as it is often implied in a false idea of 'scientific' objectivity, synonymous with detachment, with absence of interest and care. . . . How could the aims of inquiry be formulated except by reference to the interests of man? *Objectivity does not mean detachment, it means respect.* (Fromm, 1947: 111)

We have reached the current point of absurdity because we have held the value of detached objectivity to be so sacred. We wanted to have a system of knowledge where we could remove the human from the picture, look at the world objectively and have the universe tell has what to do. Well, you just can't do that. The assumptions you make to start out with influence what you see and how you shape the world. However, *relativity goes away when we put the human back into the picture.*

The postmodern dilemma is that our journey to find the truth has revealed that truth is a matter of perspective. It depends on where you start. So where do we start?

Oddly, August Comte provides the answer. He knew what was involved in founding a Science of Humanity. It is the same answer Lester Ward, Robert Lynd, Erich Fromm and Abraham Maslow would give. As Ernest Becker argues, Comte coined the word positivism so he ought to be able to define it: "By his own definition, Positivism meant *the subordination of politics to morals* (1848, p. 420). Science enters the picture *only to provide the basis for an agreed morality.*" (Becker, 1968: 45) (*Italics Original*)

What is good for the human interest? What is good for human well being? That would be our politics and our ideology.

Sociology is about coming to a moral agreement about how to create a better world. The ultimate purpose of sociology out front is to be political. Many today would beg the question: "Nah, we shouldn't do that." But as Comte knew, this is the whole purpose of sociology. Sociology would fashion an active, explorational science of society which would change the world. We have too long embraced what one observer termed "the split between mind and politics" (Alfred Weber quoted in Becker, 1968: 54)

Politics is all about direction. In which direction do human beings thrive? Which way is progress? A science of humanity—a sociology as the early sociologists saw it—is very simple. We use science (knowledge) so we can agree on values. Then we act on those values. What is good for people?

The Crucial Issue of Our Time

Look, the Enlightenment tradition is simply this—that we can come together and fashion an agreement about what makes sense from a human perspective and then create a better world based on that knowledge.

Can interventions make things worse? The answer is yes. But that does not mean we should give up hope on any intervention. There is some knowledge human intelligence can apply to make a better world.

Until We the People come together and fashion an agreement about a human agenda, we lose. Until we are willing to stand up for such an agenda, then democracy will give way to tyrants, freedom will be ousted by bullies, love will be ravaged by fear, and knowledge will be but the play thing of spin doctors. Court rooms of law and scientific gatherings will be polluted by those who sell their services to the highest bidder. Religion will become the refuge of scoundrels who promote hatred, intolerance and selfishness. And public education will be left to the propagandists and conservative think tanks. Until we create a science of Humanity based on what we know about human needs, human purposes, and human behavior, we are lost in the postmodern dilemma.

Beyond Bias

Biases are concerns, they are special interests. All values are biases. But not all biases are created equal. Sociology should have a concern, a bias if you will—an interes —in promoting human well being.

We can temporarily step back from life in an objective stance. But ultimately, we must enter the fray. The philosopher Ortega y Gasset said there are two stances: thinking/reflection and action—and that action is intrinsically political. We must come down from the ivory tower and make our knowledge matter in the construction of the world.

Notes

1. On its website, the Heritage Foundation says its mission is: "to formulate and promote conservative public policies based on the principles of *free enterprise, limited government*, individual freedom, traditional American values, and a *strong national defense*." [*Emphasis Ours*] At the American Enterprise Institute web site, you read: "The American Enterprise Institute for Public Policy Research is dedicated to preserving and strengthening the foundations of freedom—*limited government, private enterprise*, vital cultural and political institutions, and a *strong* foreign policy and *national defense*." [*Emphasis Ours*] The Cato Institute says its purpose is to promote "traditional American principles of *limited government*, individual liberty, *free markets* and peace." [*Emphasis Ours*] By peace, you can translate the words to read: a *strong national defense*.

Chapter 3:

The Human Agenda
Values and Priorities

When we look at human behavior *from any human standpoint,* a set of conclusions emerges. What confuses the issue is social scientists have enshrined objectivity as the top value and refuse to seriously consider anything else. Objectivity begins by separating human values and purposes from a science of behavior. If we put the human back in, relativity vanishes and we are set to build a Science of Humanity.

It is strange how otherwise reasonable people are so dogmatically attached to being value-free no matter in how absurd a position it places them. If we employed the least amount of common sense, we could easily come up with the values of a human agenda. From any human standpoint, some things are better. But having twisted in this scientific straight jacket, we have come up with some strange contortions.

It is easy to rate things on the basis of money. . . . more is more and less is less. But is that the only continuum on which we can agree to evaluate? We could ask, which is preferred: love or hate? life or death? to be productive, alive, creative. . . . or bored? to be healthy or sick? happy or sad? Empirically we must take it as fact that people value some things over others.

Objectivity does not mean to refrain from ever making conclusions. Having examined the evidence, there are things we can say about the conditions in which human beings thrive.

There are a variety of different ways we can proceed to build a Science of Values and they all get us to about the same territory. We could explore the living conditions of those who feel that life is good. What is associated with those who feel life stinks? If we ask people, there are certain things human beings across cultures tend to agree to call good. We can also note that there certain things they tend to typically view as bad.

We could start with human needs. The many early sociologists thought that once they had identified fundamental human needs, they would have the foundation for their Science of Humanity. Viewed that way, most of this essential work of social science has already been accomplished. We know a great deal about human needs and motivation.

If we honesty discuss what we know about living, then the following are some of what we know. It is easy to have a Science of Humanity if we start with the human. Once we have an agreement on values, then we can fashion a world around them.

Human Needs

Good for what? Good for people. Human well being should be our referent. As the early sociologists knew, the social forces are human needs and purposes. The lesson of human history and sociology should be abundantly clear: societies that do not meet human needs have greater social problems. Human systems should meet human needs. That should be a core value of a humanistic perspective.

While your list of essential needs might not be that same as mine, we will cover the same territory: meaning, empowerment (to be effective), love (response), recognition, security, physical needs (food and shelter).

You can do anything to people but you can't do it without consequences. It should be a fundamental lesson for managers and social planners. Erich Fromm summarizes:

> Some anthropologists . . . have believed that man is infinitely malleable. At first glance, this seems to be so. . . . Indeed, man can do almost anything, or, perhaps better, the social order can do anything to man. The "almost" is important. Even if the social order can do everything to man— starve him, torture him, imprison him . . .this cannot be done without certain consequences which follow from the very conditions of human existence. . . . If man were infinitely malleable, there would have been no revolutions . . . . But man, being only *relatively* malleable, has always reacted with protest against conditions which make the disequilibrium between the social order and his human needs too drastic or unbearable. (Fromm, 1968: 61–62) (*Italics Original*)

The human will get out—one way or the other. We either address human needs directly or we get unintended consequences and social problems. Social systems should meet human needs or we need to go back to the drawing board.

Happiness/Self Esteem

The idea of a Science of Human Happiness would certainly send the objective value-free scientist running for cover. But this is precisely what Aristotle had sought. He proposed both a Science of the Polis—a science of community—and a science of human happiness.

It is not non-empirical to ask people about values. What produces Quality of Life, the good life? Are there ways of living that human being prefer?

People prefer happiness to unhappiness. Let us take that as a value. Philosophers from Aristotle to Spinoza have held happiness is evidence of a well lived life. Ernest Becker (1968) once suggested self esteem—a subjective feeling of well being—should be the framework on which to integrate the disciplines. Our standard of evaluation should be the human. Human beings need to feel good about themselves.

Promoting human welfare results in fewer long term social problems. Happy people do not create many problems. Conservatives believe everyone should fend for themselves and government should not be about social solutions to promote human well being. However, Sociology certainly has the facts to

demonstrate it is both more effective and less expensive to approach human well being directly.

The Major Religions Agree on the Key Value

We could ask the great religions, what is Good? They all testify that the key to successful living is the Golden Rule. You shouldn't do something to someone you wouldn't want them to do to you.

Asking the great religious traditions is empirical. Their evaluations of the fundamental wisdom for successful living is based on collective experience. This is not in response to some survey we have sent out. These are people who have testified to it even at death's door as what is worth keeping and remembering of life.

All the great humanitarian religions—Judaism, Christianity, Islam—are based on the Golden Rule. We can say people will never come to an agreement about values. And yet across the great expanse of cultures and human history, so many different religious traditions have arrived at exactly the same fundamental wisdom. It is the precise point on which to begin to fashion a meeting of world civilizations. Only in the absurdity of a science committed to a value-free ethic would we even question the wisdom of such an ecumenical synthesis.

To put the Golden Rule in other terms: Empathy is the core of civilization. Mead's Generalized Other is a very different organizing principle for social control than the authoritarian idea of obedience. Freud in Civilization and Its Discontents had claimed society and the individual are in fundamental opposition. It is the heart of the conservative political philosophy—that society must control the individual. Social Psychology originated to articulate what Freud had missed. And what Freud has missed was the whole nature of the social. Self and Community are inseparable. You can't have the best of either unless you have the best of both. Scientific sociologists have taught George Herbert Mead as a remote concept in social psychology. However, Mead didn't see it that way. He saw the Generalized Other as fundamentally *political* in nature. He thought that groups who could be taught to develop a "generalized other" would then transform society and realistically address social problems.

The conservative position is that Political Theory (force) and Economic Theory (selfishness) theories explain human behavior and there is no need for anything else. Economists do a weird calculus where they value everything by wealth. Somehow pursuit of private greed becomes the prime motivator in their economic systems. However, self interest and selfishness are not the same thing.

Philosopher David Hume is famous for demonstrating that science will never establish final truths about how to live. He then turned his attention to the crucial question about how we know about how we should live. In what he considered his major work *An Enquiry into Morals,* he concluded that there are two sources of morality—and from these all morals follow. The first is enlightened self interest. We are drawn towards it. The second is that as Hume put it, the misery of others makes us feel "uneasy."

We could begin with a common value of empathy (there but for fortune go I) and use it as a crucial component in our method of designing a better world. Charles Cooley had recommended "sympathetic introspection" as the method of sociology. Max Weber's verstehen method could be translated to mean a sympathetic understanding.

Under What Conditions Do People Experience Life as Good?

Under what conditions do people conclude that people are good? under which living conditions do they conclude people are bad? in what conditions do people say the world is good or that God (or Nature) is good? That is also about as empirical as you can get. The only reason we can't see it is because we are committed to the pretense of this ridiculous perch of objectivity.

From any human standpoint, some things are better than others. And human beings readily testify to this if you only ask. Let's ask. Is life good? Do they say life stinks? Are people happy? Or do most feel life just hard and then you die? What do they report?

Anthropologist Ruth Benedict did precisely this and noticed patterns. In some cultures people experienced life as good. People said the world was good and indeed they also had fewer social problems and more of the consequences we would routinely define as good. In what Benedict would label synergistic cultures, people tended to have loving Gods and say it was a friendly universe.

In *The Farthest Reaches of Human Nature,* Abraham Maslow who had worked with Benedict asked: how would you feel if you woke up in the middle of the night realizing God was in the room? To some, God is love and they expected feeling awe and splendor. Others responded in fear that a judgment day of reckoning was at hand. Is God love? Is God basically vengeful? Are the gods capricious tricksters? Is the universe ruled by benevolent forces or malevolent forces (or random forces and quirks that are entirely indifferent to human fate)?

Would it be fair to say that the conditions under which people say life is good are a preferred value and could be called the Good?

Human Nature as a Self Fulfilling Prophecy

The classic debate between liberals and conservatives is over whether human beings are basically good or evil. People who experience life in different cultures reach different conclusions. To what extent is human nature a self fulfilling prophecy?

But what are the consequences of assuming people are basically good? What are the consequences of deciding they are evil? This is certainly empirical.

There are some people who will fail no matter how many chances they are given and some who make it despite impossible odds. But most of us could go either way. What if we were to take life in our hands and try to shape society so more people were good? North Dakota which has the lowest recidivism rate for juvenile delinquents in the nation begins asking one question: what kind of person do we want at the end? They then shape their juvenile system around love and helping the youth succeed.

Ruth Benedict (1970, 55) noted in synergistic cultures, people never give up on others. In other cultures, at the first sign of sin, they are ready to throw the person away: See, I told you so. Cultures that see human nature as bad have different social arrangements than cultures that conclude human nature is good. And there are quite different outcomes.

Most people want to do good. What if we took that as a key? What if we gave people the resources to do good? Even terrorists are avenging past wrongs. In even the most perverted lives, if you look closely you can still see a twisted struggle to somehow make things better.

Human nature tends to be a self fulfilling prophecy. If you design cultures as if people are good, that tends to be what you get.

Increasing the Outcomes People Already Define as Good

What things do people define as good? Under what social conditions do people find these in high supply? Under what kind of circumstances are they scarce?

We need to realize things come in clusters. As Erich Fromm notes, you have to choose packages, you can't just pick out parts:

> which of these possibilities seems preferable: the alive, joyful, interested, active, peaceful structure or the unalive, dull, uninterested, passive, aggressive structure?
>
> We deal with structures and cannot pick out preferred parts from one structure and combine them with preferred parts of the other structure. . . . Indeed, what most people would like is to be aggressive, competitive, maximally successful in the market, liked by everybody and at the same time tender, loving and a person of integrity. Or, on the social level, people would like a society which maximizes material production and consumption, military and political power and at the same time furthers peace, culture and spiritual values. Such ideas are unrealistic, and usually the 'nice' human features in the mixture serve to dress up or hide the ugly features. Once one recognizes that the choice is between various structures, and sees clearly which structures are 'real possibilities,' the difficulty in choosing becomes greatly reduced and little doubt remains which value structure one prefers. (Fromm, 1968: 95–96)

Strategies and Consequences:

One may contend values are relative but once one has decided upon a goal, the effectiveness of various strategies can be evaluated. For example, we may agree that teenage pregnancy is undesirable. The question then can be empirically solved. We can evaluate what is effective. "Just say no" can be your birth control strategy. However if that is your strategy, you are probably not going to purchase any method of birth control. It is precisely those people who end up pregnant. We should note that half of all teenage pregnancies occur within six months of first intercourse. Most of these are girls who fully intended to use "Just say no" as their method of birth control. But as teens for generations have learned, in the heat of passion many change their minds. One of the consequences of relying upon "Just say no" as a strategy is that the United States has the highest teenage pregnancy rate of any modern nation.

As literary analyst Denis De Rougemont summarized in *Love in the Western World*, it has been our dramatic luck to have chosen to try to oppose passion with tools foredoomed to foster it. Myths aside, more open cultures like Sweden have the lowest rates of teen pregnancy while the United State's repressive atmosphere rewards us with the highest rate as well as the earliest age of first intercourse and the highest number of sexual partners. As a strategy, the consequences of "Just Say No" do not work effectively. However, "Just Say No" has become the conservative all purpose solution to social problems from sex to drugs to gangs.

The literalism of mind over matter may look good on paper but it just doesn't work out that way in real life. New Year's resolutions often don't come true. Sociology takes us into the realm of realistic pragmatism evaluating strategies and the actual consequences.

What is Healthy? Preferring Life Over Death

> Under some conditions people flourish. Under others,
> although the spirit is willing, people atrophy.
>
> —William Du Bois (2001a)

Erich Fromm notes, our key value should be producing life-enhancing social systems rather than destructive, death producing ones.

> The value system corresponding to the point of view presented in this book is based on the concept of what Albert Schweitzer called "reverence for life." Valuable, or good, is all that which contributes to the greater unfolding of man's specific faculties and furthers life. Negative or bad is everything that strangles life and paralyzes man's activeness. (Fromm, 1968: 94)

Some pure logician may want to argue that masochists prefer pain and abuse — that for them pain is pleasure. It seems absurd to have to argue against such a compulsive literalism but many have been blinded by rationality and science. There are certainly extreme social conditions where people turn things upside down but anyone who routinely prefers death over life in all circumstances has come from a pretty unhealthy experience. Healthy people prefer life. We should take that as our starting point. There is something wrong with social conditions in which people come to prefer death over life.

What kind of things are related to suicide? We could make a list: hopelessness, terrorists seeking revenge as martyrs, people who feel opportunities in life are blocked. Fromm wrote:

> I want to submit, mainly for theoretical grounds, that one may arrive at objective norms if one starts with one premise: that it is desirable that a living system should grow and produce the maximum of vitality and in-

trinsic harmony, that is, subjectively, of well-being. . . . The validity of norms would follow from their function in promoting the optimum of growth and well-being and the minimum of ill-being. (Fromm, 1968: 96)

If the strict logician wants to argue that "preferring life is healthy" is a circular, they are technically right. But take your pick. Under healthy circumstances, life is better than death.

Social Problems—What Is Bad?

Somehow, "value judgment" has become a forbidden word. But we should take as our first clue that people tend to prefer some things to others. Most human beings would agree that some consequences are preferable to others.

What is Bad? What things are considered social problems? Societies have an amazing sense of agreement about what is not desirable. Murder is not a preferred pattern. Suicide tends to be a bad thing—people believe under normal circumstances, it is better to prefer life over death. And yes, there are extreme circumstances where people choose death over life—but those are not the ideal or preferred situation. We can arrive at substantial agreement about what is good just by considering what societies agree upon as being bad.

Sociologists teach in classes that social problems are socially defined. For example, doctors originally encouraged patients to smoke cigarettes because they thought it was an aid to digestion. Later smoking became a social problem. Alcohol was defined as a social problem in the early 1900s and now has been related to being seen more as an individual problem—the person is an alcoholic whose body is predisposed to not be able to handle alcohol (a fortunate convenience for the manufacturers of alcoholic beverages who can then encourage all others to drink).

Are there any social problems we would agree are universally are problems? What is bad? Murder is a place to start. Definitions of what is murder may vary from culture to culture. There are societies such as ancient Romans where women and children were defined as property which could be disposed of at will. Some of this still exists in Brazil and parts of India and Pakistan were a husband can dispense with a wife who has committed adultery. Sick as it is, this is a battle over equality. Are women and children persons or are they chattel? Societies agree that full citizens should not kill each other without socially justifiable reasons. Empirically societies with high state sponsored violence tend to have high interpersonal violence, and vica versa. But we can surely agree that ideally it would be preferable if societies had less violence.

Violence is precisely where Ruth Benedict started. She found cultures with low violence had social arrangements which structured win-win solutions whereas violent society created win-lose situations. Again, in the synergistic societies, people experienced life as good while in the non-synergistic societies where people could only get ahead at another's expense, people defined it as bad.

The Sociology of Evil

The creation of nuclear weapons gave us the ability to destroy our world in its entirety. From that moment forward, there was no human problem more pressing than the study of human evil.

—Ken Swain, The Ernest Becker Foundation listserv

Ernest Becker in *The Structure of Evil: An Essay on the Unification of the Science of Man* says that evil turns out to be a complex response to the coercion of human powers and a sterility of human meanings.

We need a world of meaning. Instead we promote common denominator values where everybody is supposed to fit and obey. There is no room for diversity.

According to FBI statistics, one out of three girls have been sexually molested. What do they think when the paragons of virtue who chant "just say no" in school? It must make little sense and must add to their internal guilt. Few are going to go to authorities and admit what has been happening, but outside the classroom, they drift towards others whose conversations and experience makes sense to them. People gravitate to others whose worldview helps them make sense of their experience. It is no accident that so many strippers and actresses from the world of pornography come from a background where they were sexually abused as kids.

Drugs and alcohol help soothe the pain. They help you drop inhabitations and communicate your pain to others from similar experience. They also provide an offstage support group to whom you can reveal your darkest secrets.

The experience of child molesters usually includes having been themselves molested when they were a child. It is a weird version of self invented psychodrama where they can now switch roles. The victim becomes the perpetrator. They can relive the experience and get in touch with and deal with their feelings—only now they have some sense of control, and the screams and panic filling the air are no longer their own. They can go at their own pace and let the memories come back gradually in a way they can try to understand them and integrate them into their lives.

To be sure, it is a perverse ritual. It is sick. But we must seek in our own humanness to develop empathy to understand how it could have been me. How would I have acted? Would I have told (or even remembered)? And how would I have tried, consciously and subconsciously, to work the feelings out? So many put themselves back in the same drama, that same vulnerable situation which they knew as a youth—only now they are in control. It is like the [child who tries to master the fear of the rollercoaster by getting back on one more time.]

And in time they may come to like it . . . to enjoy the guilty pleasures and to slowly begin to sympathize with dear old Dad and begin to understand why he did as he did. It is a [game/script] to which people feel captive as they watch from the ceiling suspended as it were viewing their own actions.

Is this all to remote for you not to understand? I am human, and nothing that is human is foreign to me. Can't you feel the feelings? Can't you begin to understand? It could have been you. And it could have been me. In *The Art of Loving*, Fromm quotes Goethe: "I am human and I can imagine of no action that I cannot imagine myself to be the author." If the circumstances had have been different and that had have happened to me. Charles Cooley had thought sympathetic introspection should be the method of sociology. It is similar to Weber's idea of Verstehen.

We need to understand the cycle of violence, abuse, and prison. Many lives are open wounds. Rather than just blaming the individual, we must change the situation. Mandating people with broken lives pull themselves up by their own bootstraps produces less than satisfactory results.

We know great deal about how to improve society. We know that the insane strategies proposed by conservatives turn the world into perpetual war. We know the war on terrorism ironically fertilizes the very roots of terrorism. We know that the war on evil actually creates evil. We know the war on crime—locking 11 times as many people up today as in 1970—has succeeding in producing *more* crime and has not addressed the social roots that cause crime. We know an agenda of greed and selfishness is not a successful strategy for realistic self fulfillment. An agenda of greed where government works to make sure the rich get theirs while making everyone else fend for themselves produces a win-lose society with extreme social problems including crime, drugs, apathy, boredom, wars and even terrorism.

Only Win-Win Solutions Need Apply

Losers create all sorts of problems; only win-win solutions need apply. Today, this is true not only locally but globally. It is true for crime and terrorism. Conservatives and pseudo liberals would like to ignore what we know about human behavior. But in a world where 97% of the world's resources go to supporting the lifestyles of 30% of its people, we are asking for trouble. The other 70% of the world's people are not going to be long content subsisting on the remaining 3% of the world's resources.

Put simply, losers are dangerous. They are always waiting for next season to get even. Pope John XXIII said, "If you want peace, work for justice." There is no clearer formula. Win-win situations are not religious pie in the sky. They are the heart of a good business deal. And they are the only rational formula for a lasting world peace. King of the Mountain is a dangerous game. And when you are on top, you'd better listen to the voices on the bottom. If a bunch of greedy human animals horde to increase their wealth, power, and status while other human animals don't have food and clean water, we are asking for wars and terrorism. We are going to have to find better ways to satisfy the human needs for status and power as well as for hunger and clean water. But we are like children lost in the maze. We refuse to look up and see the patterns.

Empirically we can show that if there are extreme gaps between winners and losers, we are asking for problems. For example, ending world hunger isn't charity. If a bunch of greedy human animals horde to increase their wealth, power, and status while other human animals don't have food and clean water, we are asking for wars and terrorism. We are going to have to find better ways to satisfy the human needs for status and power as well as for hunger and clean water.

Kant's ideal was "Maximum Individuality within Maximum Community." We want the best of both worlds. And we maintain that the evidence demonstrates that that is the only way we will ever be able to successfully accomplish either. A community only matters if it is a place where I can be myself. It is not a matter of sacrificing ourselves by being stuffed into community. We have all been in relationships where we sacrificed self for relationship and after we have warmed ourselves by the fire, it has always been a heavy price to pay with dire consequences and side effects.

This is Ruth Benedict's great genius. She sketched this territory. A culture's belief in the goodness of God, the goodness of human nature, reports of self happiness, feelings of whether life is good—these are all empirical. We can ask.

Communication—Taking Each Other Into Account

Our ends must be our means. The problem with most utopias that became nightmares is that people had a dream and then tried to impose it. We may never get to the New World but we must head in that direction. Ultimately, all we may know is our means. How do we want to travel?

George Herbert Mead's philosophy was eminently political but we have censored the real Mead because it doesn't fit the contrivance of a value free sociology. The Golden Rule—there but for fortune go I—is democracy; it is listening to others and taking them into account. Democracy is a social experiment. The Enlightenment led to the idea that reason could be used to improve human life. The physical sciences turned to the material world. The social disciplines went straight for the human potential—the perfectibility of man. Thomas Jefferson and Ben Franklin were both going over to France and sitting in the classroom with French social theorists. If you think about, the American Revolution and the new United States democracy was really an experiment in applied sociology. It was only when the revolutions had been routinized and failed to reach their full potential that they came indoors to found a science of human behavior—first in France following the bloody politics of the French Revolution which inspired Comte to dream of an orderly society, then in England and Germany where Marx dreamed of a way to overcome the sterility and oppression of the factory, and finally in the United States in the late 1800s when democracy was being ransacked by the greed of the robber barons and industrialists.

Exactly two months before September 11, 2001, Congressman Dennis Kucinich of Ohio introduced a bill to create a Cabinet-level Department of Peace to promote nonviolent conflict resolution both domestically and internationally. At first blush, it seems naive—just more posturing. But if you think about it, why shouldn't we actively be exploring peace on a cabinet level. A Department of Peace would have been a real Homeland Security Department with the power to shape a better world both here and abroad. But in the politics of fear, ultra conservatives could only imagine surveillance, police state tactics and military might as the only ways to keep us safe. Instead, we could explore non-violent alternatives, prevention, promoting the human potential. Why should war being taken seriously as a real thing of substance by serious people and peace not even be at the table?

Humanistic Science—Interest vs. Curiosity

Erich Fromm in *The Art of Loving* says there are two ways to try and uncover the secrets. One is to tear it apart. The child tears the wings off the butterfly. I wonder what if. Science would get to its core by analyzing by dissecting to its roots. But when we simply tear the butterfly apart, we find it laying dead in our hands. The butterfly that we loved no longer flies about our garden. Tearing its wings off failed to reveal its secrets and the child leaves the butterfly discarded on the ground. Its crumbled wings no longer even fitting for mounting in a scrapbook. We have not succeeded in understanding what makes it tick.

The other path is love and respect. We value our subject. We respect what we are studying and want to know it as it is—on its own terms. This is Erich Fromm's crucial distinction between curiosity and interest.

If I am interested, I must transcend my ego, be open to the world, and jump into it. Interest is based on activeness. The interested person becomes interesting to others because interest has an infectious quality, which awakens interest in those who cannot initiate it without help. The meaning of interest becomes still clearer when we think of its opposite: curiosity. The curious person is basically passive . . . . Curiosity, by its very nature, is insatiable, since aside from its maliciousness, it never really answers the question, Who is the other person. (Fromm, 1968: 85-86)

Idle curiosity wonders what it would be like if . . . ? I wonder what would happen if I tear off the butterfly's wings? Remember the early psychologists in the late 1800s had gotten prisoners volunteer to live suspended in vats of oil. As the prisoner's body gradually decomposed gradually with skin and tissue rotting out from under him, the head remained talkative on top. Scientists thought they were researching and observing the mind-body split.

Science can mask horrible cruelty. The Nazi concentration camps provided the opportunity for German scientists to conduct experiments which would have been outlawed under other circumstances. The Tuskegee experiments in the United States mirrored the same kind of scientific curiosity. Are we going to say there are no values—that the mindless tinkering of the experiments in the Nazi concentration camps were alright?

We must begin to fashion a science of human values. Or are we prepared for the atrocities of a value-free science? We begin by paying attention to the human, by caring about the human. Interest means we are involved, concerned. We *should* have a human bias. We have a stake in the human experiment.

Empowering rather than Enslaving

Robert Lynd said it so clearly: *Knowledge for What?* At the 1968 American Sociological Association meeting, the Radical Sociology Movement adopted the slogan "Knowledge for Whom." (Fuller). Ten years later, Alfred McClung Lee whose disenchantment with the sociological establishment had earlier led to his founding two groups (first SSSP and then AHS), wrote a book of the same name: *Knowledge for Whom?* It is a core question. Should the study of society be about empowering or enslaving? Are we here to make a better world or are we here to serve the interests of the ruling class? It is the question that arises once we move past a value-free science is: what do we stand for? Whose side are we on?

The are the key question for applied sociology: are we about empowering people or perfecting the art enslaving? Whom do we serve? The first answer for a humanistic sociology should be quite simply: We are for the human — we are for people.

For a sociology that doesn't think its task involves going anywhere, values are not important. But if we believe in an applied sociology then the questions "applied by whom? for what?" becomes important. Many applied sociologists today seem to think that the answer is "by whoever will give us money to do whatever it is they want us to do." Refusing to detail our values as a discipline turns us into prostitutes who go to the highest bidder. That tends to be the powers that be. Grants tend to have the values already programmed in. But to fix the problems of society may require quite different directions than the currently fashionable political agenda. But pop cures get all the grant dollars and recipes that might affect a solution or prevent problems in the first place often go begging. Managers and owners hire us to fix the problem they have designated. However, as any good consultant knows, the client's definition of the problem is often part of the problem.

Chapter 4:

The Progressive Agenda

Positive Social Change

The early sociologists believed in human progress—that sociology should be an active force in moving us towards the positive. This was the whole point of the discipline.

Knowledge for What? The answer should be: to make a better world. As Kenneth Boulding would put it, social science is about *Human Betterment.* It is the Enlightenment dream. Remember August Comte's definition of positivism—"the subordination of politics to morals." We would use politics to fashion a better society. For an applied sociology, politics is our laboratory.

If we would fashion a human agenda, our ideology might look like this: Human happiness and self esteem—a subjective feeling of well being—is an important evaluation of any program or society. We would strive to discover ways to increase human happiness and decrease human woes. Only win-win situation in the long run are practical.

Selfishness and Greed vs.
Self Esteem and Enlightened Self Interest

Conservatives see social science only as keeping people down or stimulating economic behavior. In most senses, conservative thinking about society is non-sociological. They emphasize a political science view of society (deterrence—keeping people down by force) or a narrow version of economics(rational choice (cost-benefit analysis). Their psychology is straight from Freud's *Civilization and Its Discontents* emphasizing an authoritarian version of society repressing innate anti-social human instincts. When conservatives turn to sociology, it is to functionalism which gives eminent domain to the social system over the rights and needs of the person.

When conservatives talk about the individual and society, they flip flop between all or nothing. Either the individual should be totally free or in the next breathe the individual should be totally subservient. If we value the person, then that is a naive sociology. As Cooley, noted, the individual and group are two sides of the same coin. There is a twin frontier on the human potential—it is the self and it is community. We need to follow Kant's vision of the ideal society being one that maximized both self and community.

Realistic self fulfillment demands a commitment to both self and community. Without a context, the individual cannot thrive.

Comte's vision was to discover the true laws of human behavior and then help the rulers rule with them. How do we create a society in which people are drawn towards the good? It must be a practical good rather than a short term good that disappoints—once you have it, you don't want it anymore, or a good which is accomplished at another's expense. In a phrase, we are into a conversation about enlightened self interest.

Sociologists take a situational approach to explaining human behavior. Unless we must change the situation, we can hope for little success either from terrorism or other social problems. Broken lives and despair creates social problems worldwide.

Individual troubles are often manifestations of social problems or as Karen Horney said it, individual neuroses occur along the lines of cultural strain. The most effective way to solve individual problems is often by creating social resources individuals can us in their struggles.

We must also note that people are not just selfish. We also love. And our welfare and esteem is tied up with the fate of others.

We can make the world in the image of values of greed. We call it self interest and incentive but is not self interest, it selfishness. And as an incentive, insatiable wealth that only cares about more and about insatiable power is not healthy. It is neither a goal towards which we should strive nor a trait which we should indulge. But in our age, Scourge has a new press agent and has reinvented himself. Conservatives have used techniques of propaganda to successfully marginalize the sociological perspective. Clever public relations firms play to the prejudices and fears of the masses to manipulate public opinion.

Perfecting the Art of Enslaving:
The Tragedy of Sociological Success

Sociology's profound influence on society has gone unheralded. Sociological theories dominate in organizations and even prisons. Managing customers and voters by market research have become commonplace. Goffman's impression management dominates the current political landscape as spin doctors manage appearances. It is the con artist packaging an agenda to sell. It is pretense, posturing, image without content. Even postmodernism's alienation from truth is echoed from the supermarket tabloids. Value-free pollsters join whichever side or company pays the most. Our style of thinking about society and doing sociology leaves a legacy of which we cannot be proud.

> Social science is an integral part of national life, but instead of guiding it according to a vision that would liberate the human spirit and assure the progressive development of persons, most of it is, instead, uncritically in service of the highest cash bidder. (Becker, 1971: 41)

A key question that differentiates conservatives from liberals: Are people to be controlled or empowered? How that gets answered depends upon a fundamental difference in world views. If people are empowered, do they strive for good or are they intrinsically evil?

Our answer has much to do with people's model of success. If people prefer a win-lose model, then we are doomed to empower one group of losers only to have them turn into the next generation's oppressors. Only when we rise up and understand the nature of the game are we able to see and fashion a better alternative—and that alternative is to see win-win solutions as the only practical long term alternative. Anything else simply sets up a circulation of elites.

The critical paradigm question echoes in our ear: *Knowledge for Whom?* Whose side are we on? The temptations of the world are great for a sociology trying to gain respectability and provide people with a living.

If we are to take sociological knowledge and apply it, for what purpose? To make money? Too many of today's sociologist by their methods are on the side of economics and maximum profits or the side of force, ego and authoritarianism.

In a value free stance abandons the human consistency and knowledge is just raffled off to the highest bidder. A social science which does not contend is little more than the hand maiden of the powers that be. If we are only mercenaries purchased by the higher bidder then sociology is a dark science better left undone. An earlier age called using power to get people to do things they did not want to do "black magic." (Empowering people to live their dreams and heart's desire is "white magic.")

If sociology serves the human good, if sociology is *for* people, then sociology must stand up and publicly teach what we know. How do we solve social problems? How do we create the good society?

How Should People Be Managed and Governed?

Somehow nationally we have gotten into this absurd conversation about big government vs. less government. Instead the discussion should be about good government vs. bad government. What is effective and helpful? What is a meddling nuisance?

In its Preamble, it says the United States Constitution was written in order "to form a more perfect Union, establish Justice, insure domestic Tranquility, provide for the common defense, promote the general Welfare, and secure the Blessings of Liberty to ourselves and our Posterity."

Conservatives say "promote the general Welfare" was just a slip of the tongue—that they didn't mean that government should be concerned with promoting the general well being.

Indeed they would like to limit government to helping defense contractors and large corporations pursue their economic interests. They feel justice, tranquility, the general welfare and the blessings of liberty will take care of themselves.

What Is Our Vision of the Human? Should we design social systems for people or people for social systems? Are we to serve authoritarianism and social control? We could change incentives and disincentives. We could provide viable social resources. We could choose to fund and encourage things on the basis of what is good for society and not who has the biggest lobby and campaign contributors to insist that their pockets be lined.

Politics means power. We must make the distinction Nietzsche and Fromm made about the difference between "power over" vs. "power for." As Rosabeth Moss Kanter (1977: 205) says so well, "The problem of power. . . is critical to the effective behavior of people in organizations. Power issues occupy center stage not because individuals are greedy for more, but because . . . people are incapacitated without it."

Any sociology which would be relevant to people's lives must enter politics. However, unfortunately, the theater of power is always polluted by those who would seek status and power over others. There are those who like to lead (to be in power) and nothing else. But politics could be about making the good rather than greed and ego.

We must ask how we ourselves would like to be governed? What's your theory of government? What is your theory of how we should control and motivate people? It is an important question because your vision is going to determine and shape everything else we do.

The research in social psychology clearly demonstrates that rewards work better than punishments. It is the tragedy of B. F. Skinner that he did not understand rewards deeply enough because he saw quite clearly that rewards are more effective and efficient than punishments. It remained for Abraham Maslow to flesh out the whole picture of what rewards are for the human animal.

Skinner said it well: "Love is the use of positive reinforcement." A loving society invites, it courts, it offers opportunities, it empowers. An authoritarian society dictates, expending massive amounts of energy and money trying to keep the lid on—making people conform and be obedient—to fit into societies, organizations and social arrangements which do not fit their needs. It is trying to make water flow up hill. Pushes don't work very well. What pulls naturally attract people?

Politicians must realize that human needs will out. To ignore human behavior is costly and ineffective.

Following the Crowd—Pollster Democracy

Politicians must also be taught to stand up to the crowd, to speak out. Too many politicians will tell you their opinions but not until they have checked the latest public opinion poll. This is not responding to the masses or responsive democracy. It is pandering. True leaders create an audience. They address the world speaking their thoughts outloud creating a new vision and a synthesis. They invent solutions that address the needs of many different constituencies in new and creative ways.

Many politicians just want to get elected—at any price—no matter what they have to say. Real statesmen and true leaders want to implement a vision and make a better world. They care about values and offer their visions.

Resources rather than Scientific Management

We should recommend social architecture (designing an environment) rather than social engineering (manipulating behavior). Government should be about designing Participatory Resources people can utilize in their struggles.

We must always be careful of the ever popular Science of Meddling. Rather than meddling, we should be about empowering. It again, is the difference between curiosity and interest—between trusting people and coercing.

Our Ends Must Be Our Means

Where you start determines where you end up. How you look determines what you see. Any analysis of "what is" contains an implied recommendation of what "should be." Objective, value-free science is just an illusion. We say that, but we don't do anything about it.

People not objects. We should be about human betterment. If we separate observer and the object, we can treat people as objects for manipulation. Is knowledge about prediction and control? Is that when we can say we have explained something? But have we understood?

Here's the rub—we must respect people. But that means we have introduced indeterminacy in the world for we can't control the outcome. It is the parents' dilemma. We can't completely control without eliminating the humanity our children. And it is the dilemma all government.

It is the strange lesson of freedom. That is, if we really believe in freedom.

What kind of knowledge do we want? How to get another to fall in love with you if they really do want to? How do you get someone to go to bed with you if they really do want to?) Do you want to make someone do something against their will? It is what a previous age rightly referred to as black magic. Unfortunately, most of today's social science is exactly that.

On the other hand, helping someone towards their dreams is what they would be called white magic.

This is not some epistemological nuance but the very core of any world view that values the human. Abraham Maslow in *The Psychology of Science* argued that a humanistic science would include both "I-It" and "I-Thou" ways of knowing.

Martin Buber would characterize objectivity as "I-It". We look at the human as an object wondering how to manipulate and change it. This is all well and good at times. We cannot be totally immersed in process at all times. We need to step back and gain perspective. "Setting at a distance" Buber calls it.

It is amazing how sociology neglects its voices which do not confirm its reigning paradigms (either science or postmodernism). Buber was first chair of the sociology department at Hebrew University and had ongoing dialog with many political giants of his time. Yet he is characterized as a mere philosopher and lost to graduate students in today's sociology. His insights are paramount.

To Buber's view, it is a twin fold process: we must forever pull back and set at a distance in order to see but we must also be careful to always re-enter the process and be human in dialog knowing that the "it" that I temporarily set at a distance is also "thou" just like me.

George Herbert Mead had the same theology (if we dare to call it what it is). But the objective scientist has another theology which refuses to speak in such clear terms.

Chapter 5:

The Knowledge Wars

The sociological perspective takes a situational approach to explaining human behavior. Rather than just target individuals, we must change situations. The conservative approach is anti-sociological. It blames individuals for their own problems insisting people pull themselves up by their own boot straps. When problems arise from this neglect, conservatives then turn to force to keep people down.

The Conservative Agenda goes something like this:

1. Problems are caused by individuals not trying hard enough or not making moral choices. Bad choices are made by bad people. They deserve the problems they get.

2. Behavior can be best controlled with punishment and deterrence.

3. The pursuit of selfishness in the market place will solve all problems.

4. Problems not taken care of by the above ways are best taken care of by individual volunteers and church groups.

5. Anyone can make it to the top. All you have to do is work hard.

Sociology Goes to War

Sociologists who have spoken out have typically been marginalized in times of war. Jane Addams and W.I. Thomas in particular lost credibility because of their opposition to World War I. Robert Lynd would write his *Knowledge for What?* in 1939 openly criticizing a German and American sociology which fiddled as the Nazis came to power.

As a nation rushes to collective insanity, it is the duty of sociologists to stand up. However, social scientists have a history of either sitting on their hands in times of war. The rush to national loyalty and group identity threatened the very foundations of the new discipline of sociology.

The German sociologists kept their mouths shut as the Nazis came to power. German sociology was the incubator of much major sociological thought. And yet we separate this from the context of German nationalism which resulted in World War I and the coming to power of the Nazis and World War II. Hitler used sociological thought, the new science of psychological propaganda and incorporated a corrupt version of Nietzsche's superman in his vision.

By the own admission the great efforts the Institute for Propaganda Analysis involving Alfred McClung Lee among others to teach the public to recognize propaganda and not be manipulated was disbanded at the start of World War II by its own admission because they did not want to compromise the government's ability to create loyalty by propaganda in its war efforts.

In 1968, the American Sociological Association polled its members. Most were opposed to the Vietnam war but were also opposed to ASA taking a stand against it. It is this noninterventionism that is part of the value-free scientific mindset.

Today, we know about the War on Evil. History has been witness to such crusades for time immemorial. Behavioral science has abundant information that such strategies perpetuate the very evil they seek to abolish. In our times, it is absolutely crucial that professional sociologists and psychologist stand up and say in no uncertain terms that Bush's war on evil sows the seeds of terrorism.

Sociology is at its heart political. But many find it inconvenient and politically dangerous to admit this. However, if we do not present our knowledge to the public in times of crisis, then what do we have to teach? What is applied sociology anyway if it has no relevance and guidance to the important issues of our times?

At the end of World War II, many behavioral scientists sought to prevent it from ever happening again by developing a body of research from Erich Fromm's work on destructiveness to Adorno's work on authoritarianism to Milgram's studies of blind conformity. Today, many would just as soon forget all this. We mince our words—as if we have forgotten that the "F" in the "F-scale" which measures authoritarianism stands for fascism.

The War on Sociology Itself

Sociological knowledge came to the fore under the New Deal and the Great Society with the understanding that we need to invent social answers to social problems. At the same time, there has been a determined strategy to suppress, ridicule and discredit all such perspectives. It is a war on Sociology pure and simple. Conservatives would now say any attempt to move to social solutions was a bad idea. This has been their specific agenda. The elites were also more than uncomfortable with the notion that one might want to challenge or change social arrangements.

Beginning in the early 1970s, there was a concerted effort to deny the sociological perspective. Studies of student protests during the late 1960's and early 1970s showed most campus demonstrators were sociology majors. This was a fact not lost on the Nixon administration who declared war on sociology and systematically began a campaign to reduce funding to sociology departments. A media blitz the past thirty years has increasingly sought to undermine the sociological perspective. Conservative "think" tanks have been very successfully at selling their agenda of individualism. When the public is focused only on blaming the individual, the corporate power elite can manipulate the playing field to their advantage without anyone interfering. Deregulation is but a code word for allowing Big Business to do as it likes.

However, sociology is not in business to go along with the crowd. We are not teachers to simply ratify what the powers that be want to hear.

Academia

Conservatives have ranted for years about the "bias" of universities and the media against their perspective. They felt their side wasn't being adequately represented. Anything that does not reach their conclusions, they consider to be biased. For conservatives, the think tank was the perfectly way out of this dilemma. They could just fund "research" guaranteed to promote the conclusions they favored.

Here is the odd thing. Conservatives assume there are two sides and if academics in the social sciences aren't presenting results that agree with their side then they must be biased. But if we carefully examine society and the human predicament in it, the conclusions don't slice down the middle between liberal and conservative. Indeed, any real knowledge about the origin of social problems leads to progressive conclusions.

Similarly, any honest reporting about social problems presents information to the public that is very inconvenient to the conservative perspective. There are inconvenient facts for liberals too but it does not slice down the middle.

The media you will notice has agreed to frame information in the conservative framework: fear, crime, cheering for the stock market, lazy poor people and welfare cheats, government red tape, the evil of the designated villain of the year, and aspiring to the lifestyles of the rich and famous.

If we look at the human condition with any degree of actual open mindedness then conclusions emerge that offend the conservative agenda. And here's where liberals twist themselves into a rational knot. Their commitment is to stay open minded. But it should not be a commitment to never reach any conclusions. We know some things about human behavior. Social science is so inept because it realizes there are conclusions but constrained by the market place and politics, it keeps reverting to pretending there are not.

Some conservative advocates saw think tanks as a counter weight to universities. They saw them as a perfect solution to "balance" the perceived "bias" of universities against the conservative perspective. Rich corporate conservatives could fund public "education" and "research" they were assured would support their conclusions.

Having successfully confiscated reality by buying up the media and using think tanks to promote their agenda, conservatives have now turned their attention once again to trying to capture the university. They demand equal time. Any sociologist who does not recommend that the cause of poverty is laziness and the solution is for people to just try harder is obviously biased against the conservative agenda.

The conservatives are wrong. Knowledge doesn't tilt that way. Academicians wanted the truth either way it turned out. It just happens that research suggests a direction and conclusions. The conservatives want their predrawn conclusions no matter what. This is the very definition of propaganda. They insist that their views are reality (others are mere opinions) and accuse academicians being biased just as they do the media. However, the facts often don't cut down the middle. And if you take a comprehensive at what we know from the science of human behavior, the conservatives are wrong.

Turf Wars—Who Owns the Study of Human Behavior?

We can't study society without reaching some conclusions about how to improve society. However, the powers that be may very well want to suppress those conclusions. For example, how to lower crime is no secret. Criminologists have known most of it for years. W.E.B. Du Bois over 100 years ago noted how crime was reaction and revolt against social disorganization. Shaw and McKay would later document how social conditions in the neighborhood environment produced the same crime rates over a sixty-five year period of time no matter which particular individuals, ethic or racial groups lived there. Mountains of sociological research documents two conclusions: (1) crime is intimately related to poverty and (2) prison as a way to reduce crime is not very effective. This does not fit the conservative political agenda which says crime is an individual phenomena and we just need to get tough on crime.

Political science (with an emphasis on force and deterrence) and economics (cost-benefits, rational choice theory) are the conservative explanations of human behavior. They have no need for sociological explanations.

Criminology has always been a subfield of sociology and in the 1980's, it was virtually impossible to find any sociologists who agreed with the Reagan administration's simplistic views and decision to ignore social factors and get tough on crime. A whole new discipline—Criminal Justice—was invented to try and remove the study of crime from true sociology's domain. An obscure political scientist named James Wilson was suddenly promoted to national prominence. He was at Harvard even though he didn't know anything about criminology. Other obscure political scientists and economists were also suddenly promoted to national notoriety simply because they agreed with the conservative conclusions that criminals carefully calculated the costs and the benefits of committing a crime and we needed only increase punishments to decrease crime. Historically, as it turned out, the turf war wasn't completely successful and about half of criminal justice departments are still sociologically informed while about half not.

Who owns the subject of human behavior? In the 1980s, the Reagan administration decried that mental health were only an individual phenomena. Under the Reagan, the National Institute of Mental Health which is the major funding source for mental health research was ordered to cease funding any research into social causes. Karen Horney in *The Neurotic Personality of Our Time* and Erich Fromm in *The Sane Society* had argued that society can become sick.

There is also a great body of research showing clearing the social causes of mental disorders. But no more. It was strictly a political decision. If mental problems are the result of social conditions then we would have to fund social programs to effectively address them. Biochemical explanations meant we didn't have to restructure society but could simply medicate individuals with problems. From now there would only be studies of psychological and biological causes.

Individual troubles are often manifestations of social problems or as Karen Horney said it, individual neurosises occur along the lines of cultural strain. The most effective way to solve individual problems is often by creating social resources individuals can us in their struggles.

The medication of deviance is big business. Like an old time bootlegger, drug companies stay one step ahead of the law. They bring out a new generation of drugs every few years always hailing it as the breakthrough. By the time the research catches up with them and the side effects are publicly known, they will have moved on. This year's psychological wonder drugs are the next decade's Oprah Show but by that time, psychiatrists will be prescribing a new line of potions. Methamphetamine was originally promoted by the medical profession in the early 1950s. Yep, you heard right. Doctors were the ones first prescribing speed as s quick feel better drug for almost everything. During the 1950s and early 1960s psychiatrists and doctors saw no need to redefine women's roles—instead housewives were given phenobarbital (downers) to improve their mood.

Bio-chemical causes fit nicely with whatever is the prevailing ideology. Conservatives would create people for society. Strict psychological thinking allows us to ignore the system. During the 1950s, most psychologists spoke of the "Psychology of Adjustment." They taught courses on how to get people to could conform and fit into society. However, in the late 1960s and the 1970s these courses were changed to courses in the "Healthy Personality" as psychologists came to understand that good mental health doesn't mean just conforming to your particular society. Indeed, the demands of some societies are harmful to a person. Conformity may be hazardous to your mental health.

Conservatives would like to bring us full circle back to insisting on conformity. And this time, they have drugs on their side to be able to mask and repress symptoms.

Modern psychiatrists have very little training in anything but monitoring medications. The old joke told by counselors isn't just a joke anymore—"a psychiatrist is someone trained in medicine but who does not practice it and who practices psychology although they have not been trained in it."

And they certainly have no experience creating environments that produce better mental health. The 1960s and 1970s had moved towards an approach to community mental health. But this was abandoned with the Reagan administration. Reagan's demand that mental health professionals abandon anything but pharmacological approaches has been quite encompassing as psychiatrists now administer a veritable Molotov cocktail of highly addictive drugs. Insurance companies get the bill and society can look the other way pretending there are no social consequences to our decision to ignore root causes.

What are at issue here are simply the old issues —money and clout. Who gets to bill for their services? Whom do we pay to fix the problem? Who ha credibility? And who are the experts whose advice should be heeded? Psychia trists offer a pill. Sociologists would send us the bill for fixing society (and changing social conditions). Put this way, policy makers may consider psychia trists cheap at $125 an hour or more. However, it is pennywise and pound fool ish especially when we include the costs of courts, prisons, drug treatment, and waste of human productiveness. Sociology will by its very nature upset the po litical nature of things.

On the other hand, the politics of mind control have become quite sophisti cated. We can just blame the individual and ignore society. Do we as sit politely by or do we blow the whistle? Noticing that environments with high crime rates share certain characteristics is not ideology—it is good science. However, con servatives are ideological to the end. They are intent upon blaming the individ ual for social problems.

In the early days of American sociology, Mead and Cooley developed in direct reaction against the psychoanalytic model. Remember, Freud posited so ciety and self in direct opposition. However, the early sociologists showed mind and society not separate but developed in a interwoven reciprocal fashion. But today, we ignore such knowledge.

Electric shock treatments are now making a comeback with "modern" psy chiatrists It is the electrical equivalent of hitting someone over the head with a hammer. Who knows, it might work in some cases. We can probably even find some to later give testimonials: "Being hit over the head with a hammer cer tainly helped me."

The enshrinement of psychiatrists and drug companies with their batches of potions is all footlessness, but it is high priced foolishness—and it is dangerous to humankind.

Of course, it would be polite just to give psychiatry turf. We wouldn't want to create a fuss. And if we try to wrestle control from their grubby paws, it would undoubtedly cause a fight. After all they seized this territory and why would they want to give it back?

Doctors have always been gods. In the past patients asked them all sorts of advice for which they were never qualified. Now modern pharmacy puts behav ior back in medicine's grip. We can get people to adjust to society—chemically. Why would we want to have to change social arrangements?

Academic Credibility

Sociology originated to put together all of the other disciplines. As Ernest Becker noted, the new discipline of sociology was in a impossible position. It wanted academic credibility. At the same time to get that credibility it would have to rely the older disciplines (especially economic and political science). At the same time, the necessity of an extra discipline to put together all the other disciplines still remains. Comte felt that this discipline would then look at how all the other disciplines affected the human and how knowledge could be used to create progress to improve society and human welfare.

In our day, the big kid on the block has become psychiatry. The movement thirty years ago to build a Clinical Sociology is illustrative of the predicament. Sociologists wanted to be able to bill for their services just like psychologists. Licensing became an issue. Ironically, Clinical Sociologists were grandfathered in—we lost the war while a few practitioners won the battle. Today, insurance bucks go to psychiatrists. And today, even counselors are losing to drug companies and the new breed o psychiatrists who in reality little more than pharmacists

Recently, the American Psychiatric Association moved to new categories of "relational disorders" which they felt could eventually yield themselves to treatment by the new psychiatric means of mediations. People who were normal in most circumstances might exhibit specific symptoms in particular circumstances—batterers, truants, gang members. Rather than change the circumstances as sociologists would recommend, the new designation of "relational disorders" would allow them to be treated with mediations and insurance companies billed. Even more important, this would allow psychiatry to expand its turf.

Bill was recruited by Applied Sociology president Jay Weinstein and worked to draft a letter to the APA voicing our concerns. But if you think about it, the message could be simple—"butt out."

We must understand the nature of the predicament and why we must stand our ground. What is at stake is the shape of the world . . . . and the very existence of sociology. For sociology to just take its place as a routine discipline in the academy means the very core of sociology is extinguished. This is not just a petty inter-discipline squabble. What is at stake is not just our discipline boundaries but the human.

August Comte the founder of sociology had thought if there were x number of disciplines, there must be one more (x + 1) to put it all together—*and access their impact on the human.*

Sociology looks at all disciplines and their consequences upon the human. It sees economic man as but a portion of the picture, biological man only another component. Comte believed we need one more discipline (which he called sociology) to take a view of all together and how knowledge could be used to make a better world for people.

That means we are forever contending with the powers that be who are content with the world the way it is. For sociology to be an active presence transforming the world, there must forever be this tension. To sit back and comfortably solicit grants, do research, write journal articles and not make waves pleases academic deans but it makes sociology only relic of its dream.

W.E.B. Du Bois respected the traditional lines between sociology (encased in academia and science) and the real world of action. In his life, he took turns moving back and forth between the two. On the other hand Jane Addams integrated these two realms realizing sociology is intrinsically political.

The Marriage of Science and Religion

The Enlightenment began by separating values from practice. Science and the real world went one way while religion and values went the other.

We have found that all truth comes from a perspective. If you start with a premise it shapes our conclusion. Values are intimately married to perspective. Values influence what we see. That is the truth.

The division of the world into secular and sacred takes place with the separation of values from science. But if we would begin with a concern for human betterment, what would we see and what kind of world would we make? We need room for the human spirit.

Ernest Becker (1968: 273) wrote, "'higher' esthetics is precisely that; it calls more of man's spirit into play, releases more of the inner personality and brings it to bear upon the world."

> When science opted out of life and objectivized man, scientists of course lost the possibility of seeing any mystery at all in man, of seeing any heightening being, even in secular terms (Becker, 1968: 267).

> The problem, inescapably, is a social one. We have destroyed the interhuman in our time simply because we have refused to implement social forms which would liberate man . . . (Becker, 1968: 273).

Today, we coerce the spirit, manage public opinion for private corporate gain and have rendered the world into stale McDonalization cultural forms. Ernest Becker's conclusion in his study of *The Structure of Evil*, evil turns out to be a complex response to the coercion of human powers and a constriction of human meanings.

What Do We Know? Where shall we stake our lives?

Today, our image of the human is at stake. Are people potentially good or are they inevitably evil? Can we change people's situations? Or should we just blame individuals for their problems and then could out the police or military when people fail to behave? Who gets to define the causes of human woes? Can people do better? Can we make a better world? Where do we place on faith?

Conservatives would make people fit into society. Progressives say we must design society for people. There cannot really be a conservative sociology—they do not believe ultimately in the sociological. Their solutions are borrowed from political science, economics and the coercive psychology of adjustment. They do not see the need or advisability for sociological intervention to improve human welfare.

Where shall we head? What are our values? As Ernest Becker (1971: 155–156) says in *The Lost Science of Man*:

> We need to keep in view . . . the Aristotelian problem of final cause, and not merely material cause. We need to try and understand what life is all about,

where it is heading. Otherwise, we ourselves will be headless, undirected, trivial men.

By reintroducing the dimension of ontology as the ultimate ground of human freedom, our model of man and community will not be a finished model, as the critics of manipulative science so rightly fear.

the science of man, while working toward the new community, would be partly grounded in a creative new myth of the meaning of life. We would then have . . . a science of man with a vision of community, *working in a community that itself creates the new symbols of a new social order*. In other words, we would be scientists working within a living myth of the significance of our own science and of our own lives, scientists working with artists—in a sense subordinate to art because partaking of a creative mythology, as Comte's genius foresaw. In this way, and in this way alone, would our general theory of alienation have its fullest reach, since it would seek to overcome alienation not only in our 'subjects,' but in ourselves, in the community of science.

American sociology was born out of the progressive movement. What does the human heart want? Remember George Herbert Mead's vision. He felt it was empirical to note that across the course of human history has been the dream of universal community—in the idea of universal love as advocated by all the great world religions, the more secular lowest common denominator ideal of global trade between all peoples and the ideal of universal communication (that we would be able to understand both each others words and each other's behavior). This ideal is exactly the kind of creative myth Becker had in mind. It is a core value on which to found a science of humanity. It should partner with Kant's vision of the ideal—maximum individuality within maximum community—and with Buber's ideal that we must have not only "I"–"It" objectivity and technologies but "I"–"Thou" knowledge and relationships with others that respect each other as fully human. It is on these core values that we can found a Science of Humanity. We have only to begin.

Chapter 6:

Public Education

The political problem par excellence is the problem of education.
—Henri Bergson, Nobel Prize Acceptance Speech, 1927

If you haven't noticed, public education about how to change the world for the better is called politics. In our time we are witnessing a moral failure to educate. Oh, we do it around the edges. But the core of the discipline remains sterile. The crucial problem of our time is that the media has been confiscated by large corporate interests who use it predominately to promote one view. It has become such that major candidates from both parties are afraid to go outside the agenda defined by this corporate media as mainstream. How do we then do public education?

Max Weber in 1918 gave two lectures, one on "Science as a Vocation" and one on "Politics as a Vocation." Comte and Ward would have told him it is a false dichotomy. In "Politics as a Vocation," Weber discusses the "calling for politics." When one both sees "ultimate ends" and "feels such responsibility with heart and soul," a "mature person—no matter whether old or young in years—. . . reaches the point where he says: 'Here I stand; I can do no other.'"

And this is where we are today as a discipline. Conservatives have pushed the ideology of individualism so far that we must now respond or face the extinction of sociology as an active discipline.

Here we stand. We can do no other. A political agenda whose tenets are rugged individualism, as is currently popular, is the antithesis of what Erich Fromm called *The Sane Society*. From its tenets flow only social problems. Having studied sociology, we can say no other. Our science of human betterment shows the folly of a laissez faire approach focusing only on individuals. In a time when such approaches dominate the media and liberal politicians do little more than tag along, it is essential that we find ways to teach sociology to the general public.

Public education today is in the hands of Rush Limbaugh, Bill O'Reilly, Fox News, corporate media executives and the Heritage Foundation. This is how most of America gets its information. And this is how the public forms interpretations of the day's events. Unprofessional and irresponsible verbiage in the name of journalism has both taken hold in America as a source of information and at the same time defamed and demeaned the age-old honored traditional of professional journalism.

In an era of globalization, more than ever, we need a conversation about human values. What is important? On what shall we build the world?

It is hard to export democracy when you don't understand it. How do we want to be governed? How should people be managed? What kind of society should we make? and what kind of values should we embrace? What is our image of the world and the good society? This is the stuff of politics. Sociology must be about this or it is trivia.

SECTION II

BUILDING A SCIENCE OF HUMANITY

Putting All the Disciplines Together

Sociology's Answer to Sociobiology

If you haven't noticed, the whole culture is back in the late 19th century. Conservatives today are back embracing the same foolhardy theories that demanded the creation of sociology in the first place. Rugged individualism. Free Markets. Many sociobiologists today seek to strike the final nail in the coffin for left wing politics. We are told we must now argue our positions from within the framework of new found biological truths. What is at stake is the very existence of the human.

The question "what does it mean to be human?" can best be answered in the context of what we know about psychology, sociology, and existential philosophy. This section deals with the period of the birth of the idea of a science of human behavior (sociology and psychology) in the United States. Sociobiology reopens the crucial conversation about a science of humanity we have forgotten. However, it takes wrong turns submitting to the paradigm of the natural sciences rather than bridging a synthesis between the social and natural sciences. A Science of Humanity requires the inclusion of two essential components of human existence which the natural sciences so swiftly sweep from view—values and meaning.

Sociobiology takes a million wrong turns. But it does one thing that modern sociology has forgotten—it tries to put everything together. August Comte had thought sociology would put all the disciplines together asking how does each relates to the human and what conclusions for making the world can be gained from considering all together. The only adequate response to sociobiology must be a holistic answer which talks about everything. Those trained as traditional scientists may find our generalizations about life unsatisfactory but it is hard to take broad strokes without taking broad strokes. However, too much specialization can insure we never get to the broad conclusions necessary to ever found a Science of Humanity. The answer will always be eternally postponed awaiting further data.

Chapter 7 sketches what we know of human nature, human needs and about fundamental social and psychological processes. A synthesis of what we know about the human condition is necessary if we are to begin a political remaking of society based on knowledge from the behavioral sciences. Chapter 8 explores the possibility of the implementation of a true Science of Humanity where humankind takes life in its hand and consciousness knowledge intervenes as an active force in the progress of evolution and the direction of life itself. We are back to the founding arguments of social science and recovering the lost humanistic tradition which could create a Science of Humanity.

Chapter 7:

Human Nature:

Basic Needs and Processes

As Daniel Dennett writes in *Darwin's Dangerous Idea*:

> From what can 'ought' be derived? The most compelling answer is this: ethics must somehow be based on an appreciation of human nature—on a sense of what a human being is or might be, and on what a human being might want to have or want to be. (Dennett, 1995: 468)

This is the same argument August Comte and Lester Ward made more than 100 years ago. However, as anthropologist Ernest Becker (1974) noted, "One of the great obstacles to the development of a theory of human nature that would command scientific respect has been the bitter dispute between the biological and cultural scientists themselves."

Sociobiology brings us back to that grand conversation about Everything. Comte thought if there were x number of disciplines, there needed to be one more (x + 1) to put them all together as they relate to the human. He called his meta-conversation "sociology." Sociobiologists are renewing the essential work at synthesis that a cowardly, value-free social science abandoned.

Take a trip to Barnes and Noble. It will scare you to the core. The section on sociobiology/evolution is as large as the section on sociology. The public is hungry for a relevant theory that puts everything together.[1] The relativism of value-free science and postmodern philosophy have left many retreating to fundamental versions of religions in search of solutions to the basic problems of human existence. Human beings need values and a direction. Conservatives understand this and people are listening:[2] *We must begin with values because where we start influences what we shape.*

Sociology has reached its current absurdity because the values of science have been held to be so sacred. We wanted a system of knowledge that removed human values from the picture, looked at the world objectively and allowed the universe to reveal the truth about how to live. Such relativism turns out not to work. However, *relativity disappears once we put the human back into the picture.* As the early sociologists knew, once we understood human needs and human nature then (and only then) would we have the basis for a Science of Humanity.

The ultimate political turf war looms over the human. During the 1980s, the Reagan administration ordered the National Institute of Mental Health to ignore the considerable research showing social factors caused mental problems and henceforth only fund research into psychological and chemical causes. Conservatives could then avoid spending money on social programs and blame individuals for problems. Armed with the new biological research funded the past two decades, sociobiologists now claim social science is obsolete. In psychiatry, a battle now rages between traditional psychotherapy and the new breed of psychopharmacological psychiatrists who see everything as only biochemistry (Luhrmann, 2000).

New research allows us to see down to the molecular level. But how is that related to behavior? Sociobiologists today are using biological research as metaphor on which to hang their own pet theories about humanity.

Sociologists are right to be wary of the latest round of biological imperialism. We have been down this road before. It is dangerous territory fraught with wrong turns and potential abuses. The stakes couldn't be higher—our vision of humanity. A deterministic, reductionistic science seeks to explain everything away and take the mystery and wonder out of life. Becker summarizes the crucial failing of sociobiology:

> Man's fate . . . has to be an open mystery instead of a closed one.
> This is where, I think, the criticisms of the cultural anthropologist . . .
> come to rest. (Becker, 1974: 252)

Human Needs

What is right about sociobiology is they once again make us focus upon human nature and human needs. Sociobiologist Steven Pinker (2002) in *The Blank Slate: The Modern Denial of Human Nature* accuses social scientists of treating humans as infinitely malleable. He is right. There are limitations. We must discuss fundamentals. Erich Fromm's classic "What Does It Mean to Be Human?" is the best place to start. It must to be quoted at length.

> Some anthropologists . . . have believed that man is infinitely malleable.
> At first glance, this seems to be so. Just as he can eat meat or vegetables or
> both, he can live as a slave and as a free man, in scarcity or abundance, in
> a society which values love and one which values destruction. Indeed,
> man can do almost anything, or, perhaps better, the social order can do
> anything to man. The 'almost' is important. Even if the social order can do
> everything to man—starve him, torture him, imprison him, or over feed
> him—this cannot be done without certain consequences which follow
> from the very conditions of human existence. Man, if utterly deprived of
> all stimuli and pleasure, will be incapable of performing work, certainly
> any skilled work. If he is not that utterly destitute, he will tend to rebel if
> you make him a slave; he will tend to be violent if life is too boring; he
> will tend to lose all creativity if you make him into a machine. Man in this
> respect is not different from animals or from inanimate matter. You can
> get certain animals into the zoo, but they will not reproduce, and others
> will become violent although they are not violent in freedom. . . .The history of man shows precisely what you can do to man and at the same time
> what you cannot do. If man were infinitely malleable, there would have
> been no revolutions; there would have been no change because a culture

would have succeeded in making man submit to its patterns without resistance. But man, being only *relatively* malleable, has always reacted with protest against conditions which make the disequilibrium between the social order and his human needs too drastic or unbearable. (Fromm, 1968: 61–62)

We can do anything to people but not without consequences. We ignore human needs at our peril. Social systems that do no answer human needs will have all kinds of social problems.

Your list of human needs may not look exactly like mine, but they cover much of the same ground. Whether we designate limitations as biological imperatives or existential contingencies, it is important to acknowledge there are essentials fundamental to the human condition. I see no advantage to designating them as genetic except to claim turf for sociobiologists.

I have always liked Judith Bardwick's (1979) term, "existential anchors." We need to make sense of life. We also need a framework to organize and understand everyday life because unlike other animals who can become rabid, humans can go crazy (Fromm, 1968). The other key essential anchor is human contact. W.I. Thomas called the human need for intimacy the need for "response." You know you are alive because when you act, someone responds. As psychologist William James had said, no worse punishment could be designed than when you act, no one responds and when you say something, no one hears. We need response or it is as if we do not even exist. We need to be effective—babies or adults crying for help need to feel their cries can elicit a response.

Ernest Becker was probably the last great mind to synthesize the disciplines. *The Structure of Evil: An Essay on the Unification of the Science of Man* presents a theory of human ills. He would win the Pulitzer Prize for *The Denial of Death*. In what I think was the last article he himself submitted for publication "Toward the Merger of Animal and Human Studies," he says something odd. Sociobiologists are "speaking the truth 'falsely.' . . . Let us linger on this important denouement because it leads us exactly to the merger of animal and human studies."

> the general instinct of self preservation. . . . can be satisfied in any number of general ways. The enthusiastic victory over creatureliness is a phenomenological problem in sum, and in this way we have an intimate reconciliation of [sociobiology and its] critics in cultural anthropology and sociology. They are all talking about the same thing—transcendence of creature limitations. (Becker, 1974: 243–244)

The very evolution which brought intellect to consciousness gave us the knowledge we will die. With consciousness comes anxiety. We are immediately in contact with animal fears about survival. Sociobiology offers the important truth that all is not spin as postmodernism would have it. The world is not only a social construction. We are a finite animal creature. We are living. We have needs.

> the real problem of the human condition is terror of death and the need for

heroic transcendence. Scientifically we are distracted by shuffling off to the side of the problem, to flocking instincts and bonding biograms. I am reminded here of the eminent William Ernest Hocking's criticism of psychoanalysis and its focus on sexual problems: he said that these only served to distract us from the real problem of the meaning of the world and of one's life. (Becker, 1974: 251)

The Nature of Life—Biology and the Life Force

Human beings need meaning. We are back to the larger meta-conversation about life. The early scientists had been out to discover God's laws. Modern science was created with Spinoza's conclusion it didn't make any difference whether scientists used the word "God or Nature" as the ultimate final cause in their theories. However, that shouldn't have granted free license to leave out both.

David Hume would show the "secret springs" of life couldn't be dissected or known by induction. This would not do for a science out to eliminate all mystery. Immanuel Kant rushed in and "saved" Western science. He said there are noumenon and phenomenon. Noumena are metaphysical and can't be known by scientific analysis. Phenomena are the world of appearances that can be observed (and measured). Science moved merrily off to study phenomena (the world as it appears) and construct a science (and a world) just as if "secret springs" did not exist. But studying only the world of appearances doesn't get us to reality.

What are we to think of a life science that leaves out life? We must put life back into Science. There must be room for the human and the hand of life. God (or Nature) are left only as remote first principles unrelated to daily events. Fromm once commented medical students learn more about cadavers than human life. In *The Lost Science of Man*, Becker says we must be more than just "foreground manipulators."

> We need to keep in view . . . the Aristotelian problem of final cause, and not merely material cause. We need to try and understand what life is all about, where it is heading. Otherwise, we ourselves will be headless, undirected, trivial men. (Becker, 1971: 154)

The Will to Power

Where is life headed? Sociobiologist Daniel Dennett calls Nietzsche one of the first sociobiologists because of his idea of the will to power. Nietzsche's "will to power" is the same actualizing energy Abraham Maslow and Carl Rogers talked about and sometimes gets Nietzsche designated also as the Father of Humanistic Psychology. It is the idea the Army ripped off for its most popular advertising campaign "Be all you can be."

> basically the will to power in Nietzsche is . . . the dynamic self-affirmation of life. . . . It is . . . the drive of everything living to realize itself with increasing intensity and extensity. The will to power is not the will of men

to attain power over men, but it is the self-affirmation of life in its self-transcending dynamics, overcoming internal and external resistance. (Tillich, 1954: p. 36)

This is a different conception of power than we are accustomed. Nietzsche noted when most people use the word freedom, they speak as if they meant *freedom from*, but what they really desire is *freedom for*: to accomplish something. This is what feminists refer to as personal power—the ability to get where you want to go. Fromm makes the same distinction as Nietzsche terming it the difference between *power of* and *power over*. "Power over" is an attempt to overcome the impotence of being ineffective.

Power of = capacity, and power over = domination. Power = domination results from a paralysis of power = capacity. 'Power over' is the perversion of 'power to.' . . . Domination is coupled with death, potency with life (1947: 94)

The ultimate human agenda is not "power over" but "power to" make sense of our existence and feel good about ourselves. Carl Rogers (1977) says it took him a long time to understand when he was talking about self realization, he was really talking about *Personal Power*. Like the power of love or even charisma, we are attracted towards actualized being. It is no secret that people want to be happy. People strive to feel good about themselves. Is self esteem the primal force? Becker once thought perhaps self esteem—a subjective feeling of well being—would be the value on which to unify the disciplines.[3]

In their commitment to building a science of behavior, the social scientists modeled their discipline on the hard sciences model of a value free science. But the central fact we know about the human is people need values. They need to make sense of their existence, they need meaning, purposes and a frame of reference to rank alternatives and decide upon a direction. In a value free system of knowledge, human beings are lost with no direction. All that is necessary to step out of this circle of the relativism of science is to agree upon one value. Erich Fromm (1968: 96) writes:

I want to submit . . . . one may arrive at objective norms if one starts with one premise: that it is desirable that a living system should grow and produce the maximum of vitality and intrinsic harmony, that is subjectively, of well being.

The Psychology of Science—Mind & Matter

But sociobiology goes the other way modeling its synthesis after the value-free approach. Sociobiologists get Nature back into science but they claim the keys to the mysteries of life are locked deep in the genetic code. But since it is in code, who speaks for the code? Today's sociobiologists speak for Nature much as a previous generation of prophets spoke for God.

Since we have to be initiated into their club to understand the code, we need to examine club rules. Separating mind from matter—and then using our science of matter to explain mind—involves some subtle sleight of hand. The scientist steps out of life onto a platform of objectivity. We pretend science is not a human act. Mind simply views body.

It gets especially tricky when we then decide to turn methods we used to view matter back around on mind. The toolbox borrowed from the hard sciences is ultimately conservative emphasizing detachment, skepticism, predicting and controlling, an absence of values and "what is" (Hampden-Turner, 1970). All that doesn't fit the rational scientific worldview gets swept into a new category that gets invented at the same time called the "unconscious." If you didn't notice, much that is human gets chased from view. This is important to remember because sociobiologists are going to use this objective stance as the platform from which to claim their truths.[4]

Sociobiologists deem outside, objective knowledge superior to personal knowledge, feelings, and empathy. However, as Martin Buber (1957, p. 97) notes, "The principle of human life is not simple, but twofold . . . the first [is] 'the primal setting at a distance' and the second 'entering into relation.'"

'Setting at a distance' is essential: for thought, for movement, for perception, and for speaking. In order to see and frame in language, we must distance— abstract. This is the nature of thought. And yet our abstractions from whole— from process—must not be such that they are reified and become treated as the thing-in-itself. "Setting at a distance" must not be allowed to cement into objects; our framework of thought must not estrange Self from Other. It is essential that we frame our conceptions in a way that we can overcome the separateness which is implicit in our distancing and thus preserve a dialog (Buber, 1957, p. 105).

Maslow in *The Psychology of Science* says a humanistic science must include both ways of knowing—setting at a distance and getting involved. It incorporates "I–Thou" knowledge as well as "I–It" objectivity. What does it mean to be a human being? We have inside experience. To ignore this is hardly empirical.

Our methods must respect our subject matter. We cannot successfully approach the human with the same mechanistic tools we used in the hard sciences.

That which is forced must preserve its identity. Otherwise, it is not forced but destroyed . . . . One cannot transform a living being into a complete mechanism, without removing its centre and this means without destroying it as a living unity (Tillich, 1954, p. 46).

Mead also shows clearly we must treat self as an object–a "me"—in order to see. But we must also allow room in our social conceptions for the movement of the "I." By reifying a stance of objectivity, science cements the "me" but leaves no room for the "I." Freud's dictum is revealing of a scientific approach: "Where Id was, let Ego be." Science is out to territorialize and tame the mysteries. "I" must become "me." But in such a world, we are reducing to the role player looking in the mirror. It is small wonder that Erving Goffman's sociology has become the prime methodology of today's spin doctoring politics. We are reduced to images and "me's" with little room for the creative, authentic "I."

Both our social theories and our theories of organization must be reconceptualized to provide room for the "I." A science solely focusing on the "me" ultimately means the elimination of the human.

Left Brain, Right Brain

"Feelings are also knowings," philosopher Ernest Hockings said. But trusting such instincts isn't quite what most sociobiologists had in mind. The history of Science unfortunately has been the story of the left side of brain territorializing the right brain. We have separated the world into masculine and feminine and then devalued and ignored all we labeled feminine.

Psychologist Carl Jung would say the most important task of our time is to recover the feminine. Jung felt unless we recovered the feminine in all of us, society would leave behind the human and people would become sick. We need a left brain framework that respects right brain qualities. We need to organize our understandings in such a way as to allow room for the movement of the spirit and the hand of life.

Sociobiology sits back looking objectively at the genetic code without allowing us to criticize the contrived platform from which they gain their view. Susan Griffin in *Woman and Nature* writes:

> patriarchal thought . . . represents itself as emotionless (objective, detached . . .)
> This voice rarely uses a personal pronoun, never speaks as 'I' or 'we,' and almost always implies that it has found absolute truth, or at least has the authority to do so. . . . You will recognize that voice from its use of such phrases as 'it is decided' or 'the discovery was made.' (Griffin, 1978: xvi)

A humanistic perspective puts the human back in. We are more than just objects. Values and meanings are central to what makes us human. Objectivity alone will not do. We have a stake in the human experiment.

Mind is Not Just Brain

Sociobiologists talk as if mind and brain are the same. As my friend humanistic psychologist Arthur Warmoth reminds: Brain is a product of biochemistry. Mind is not. It is a critical distinction.

Just because a behavior is accompanied by chemical processes in the brain doesn't mean biochemistry caused it. If you are about to be run over by a bus, your brain will trigger a rush of adrenalin. That doesn't mean adrenalin caused your reaction. And although we can create panic by injecting a person with adrenalin in the laboratory, we have forgotten about the bus.

There are three core components to behavior: Mind-Body-Environment. Reducing one to the other is absurdity. Psychedelic drugs can approximate a mystic state of consciousness but that doesn't mean a drug induced nirvana is more than a "counterfeit infinity." The spiritual is not just a chemical reaction. (Roszak, 1969)

One could say brain comes first and mind is based on chemical processes
But human beings are born into pre-existing groups just as surely as they are
born into individual bodies. Cultural myths and patterns of thought exist well
before any particular animal. It's a chicken and egg affair.

Brain is hardware, mind is software. Everything can't be reduced to understanding hardware. Anyone who has experienced DOS compared to modern
Windows and Macintosh operating systems appreciates that software makes all
the difference in the world. In fact, it doesn't make any sense to consider one
without the other. They evolve together.

As Ward and the early sociologists knew, the social forces are human needs
and purposes. The social evolves as we act. The Sociological Perspective is this:
Human behavior takes place in a context. Culture is a series of resources. The
social resources one has available influences how one acts. Different environments make some behaviors more likely and some less probable. By seeding
resources into the environment, we can influence behavior.

Human beings are both creatures of culture and creators of culture. Dennis
Wrong had warned us of the dangers of an oversocialized viewed. We must ask
the question—what is society for? Is culture a series of social resources designed
for people to meet their intrinsic needs? Or is it the ultimate absurdity—people
made for society—people to serve the social construction?

What is mind? It cannot just be reduced to body and matter . Science does
not provide definitive explanation and eliminate mystery as we thought. We are
part of something larger. In *The Denial of Death*, Becker writes:

> Science thought that it had gotten rid forever of the problems of the soul by
> making the inner world the subject of scientific analysis. But few wanted to
> admit that this work still left the soul perfectly intact as a word to explain the
> inner energy of organisms, the mystery of the creation and sustenance of living
> matter. We still haven't explained the inner forces of evolution that have led to
> the development of an animal capable of self-consciousness, which is what we
> still must mean by "soul"—the mystery of the meaning of organismic aware-
> ness, of the inner dynamism and pulsations of nature. (Becker, 1973, p. 191)

It is a tautology to say the evolutionary step that made us human is consciousness. Surely our degree of consciousness is what separates us from other animals
but that doesn't abolish the question of what brought us to consciousness.

Henri Bergson—A Humanistic View of Evolution

We have become accustomed to thinking of religion and science as being opposites. We think back to lawyers Clarence Darrow and William Jennings Bryan
debating evolution in the 1925 trial of school teacher John Scopes for breaking a
Tennessee law forbidding teaching evolution. We forget there were also philosophers and religious people who had a quite different take on Charles Darwin
and evolution. They felt thought Darwin hadn't gone far enough.

If mankind was indeed some sort of evolved ape, how could it be that Darwin—himself an evolved ape—had managed to come up with the theory of evo-

lution? They reasoned not only bodies, but consciousness itself must be evolving. We are nature with a concept of nature. Humanity is nature's way of becoming conscious of itself.

French philosopher Henri Bergson attracted the greatest following of any public intellectual in the late 1800s and early 1900s. He was as popular then among educated people as Billy Graham is today among conservatives. Bergson was no fly by night. He would win the Nobel Prize for literature two years after Scopes Monkey trial. Bergson had a major influence on the important thinkers of his time including George Herbert Mead and the pragmatism of William James. Had James lived long enough, he was planning to write the introduction to the American translation of Bergson's *Creative Evolution* (1911).

As Mead notes, Herbert Spencer missed the point in seeing evolution as only adaptation. Bergson shows even biological evolution is also creative—it involves innovation (Mead, 1938: 506). The life force passing through matter is what Bergson calls the "élan vitale." He would later say that it is the "impetus to love." If God is love, Life begins as a speck (in the mind of God if you will). The life force pulsing through matter evolves seeking greater expression. Not only is the physical universe evolving but mind as well. This is a quite different epistemology than a mechanical God pulling the strings of the universe and laying the mystery deep in the genetic code. Human beings evolve gradually as a way of matter being able to know God, taking the universe in hand and moving closer to getting to heaven standing up. Bergson sketches a grand, majestic vision. If one wants a more contemporary version, there is nothing finer than feminist Susan Griffin's *Woman and Nature*.

> Only now, as we think of ourselves as passing, do . . . we list all that we are. That we know in ourselves. We know ourselves to be made from this earth. We know this earth is made from our bodies. For we see ourselves. And we are nature. We are nature seeing nature. We are nature with a concept of nature. (Griffin, 1979: 225–226)

In *The Two Sources of Religion and Morality*, Bergson deals with society and does a complete job of illustrating institutionalization and reification. From time to time, pioneers in morality appear who show us how to love more—a Jesus, a Buddha. We are drawn towards better.

> This is what occurs in musical emotion, for example . . . . In point of fact, it does not introduce these feelings into us; it introduces us into them, as passersby are forced into a street dance. Thus do pioneers in morality proceed (Bergson, 1935, P. 40)

> It is these men who draw us toward an ideal society, while we yield to the pressure of the real one (Bergson, 1935, p. 68).

> exceptional souls have appeared who sensed their kinship with the soul of Everyman . . . . The appearance of each one of them was like the creation of a new species . . . . Each of these souls marked a certain point . . . of a love which seems to be the very essence of the creative effort (Bergson, 1935, p. 95).

Inspiration returns us to our souls, touching us in a way we had almost forgotten. Much of Mead's "I" and "me" is similar to Bergson. As we abstract to reflection, the creative becomes reified. Moving from inspiration to formulas, followers try to convert everything to recipes to get it to happen again. It gradually turns into moral codes and social obligation. Even the most inspired insights get patterned into ritual and routine. Then there is the need for a new breakthrough to bring us back to more life once again.

Pioneers in morality show us practical ways to love more—how to create a win-win situation where everyone's needs are met. Karl Marx had concluded there is a fundamental synthesizing force moving through history. Lester Ward invented a word for the driving force behind evolution. He wanted it to convey the idea of a synthesizing energy. The word he coined was "synergy."

The Self and the Social

The early sociologists and psychologists set about the task of articulating the fundamental social processes. They thought once they understood those, they would have the foundation for their Science. The remainder of Part I explores these fundamental processes.

Much of what is wrong with sociobiology is an immature understanding of self and society. Sociobiology uses the psychology of Sigmund Freud and primitive versions of economic and political theory. Freud's classic picture in *Civilization and Its Discontents* is that society must keep down our animal natures. Working in the shadow of Darwin, Freud shocked Victorian sensibilities by insisting on grounding the core existential dilemmas in bodily functions: sexuality, weaning the infant from its mother's breast, and house breaking the little human animal. The metaphors often distracted people from what he was actually saying.

Sociobiologists don't seem to understand the actual existential dilemmas. This is critical. What Freud called the oral phase, his student Carl Jung would talk about as the individuation process. Initially infant and mother are one and whether a mother breast feeds or not, the child's sucking response is primary during the first few months of life. Indeed all the world comes in through the mouth. There is no distinction between "Me" and "Not Me." The oral phase is learning how to distinguish between what is self and what is other. Learning to make this distinction in a healthy manner is the existential dilemma of the individuation process.

The social psychology of George Herbert Mead and Charles Cooley would deepen our understanding of the social. Self and other are not fundamentally opposed as Freud would have it. The self and other are constructed with the same stroke that simultaneously sets the division between what is "Me" and what is "Not Me." Cooley would note the group and individual are but two sides of the same coin.

Social psychology originated to articulate what Freud had missed. And what Freud had missed was the true nature of the social. Sociobiology does not understand this. Mead and social psychology traced the creation of mind and society.

We become social by learning to take the role of the other. The Generalized Other is the opposite of Freud's Superego. The Superego is the logic of obedience. The "Generalized Other" is a totally different organizing principle for society. The Generalized Other maintains social order by empathy. Whereas "Superego" has to do with repressing, the Generalized Other has to do with being able to put yourself in the other's place. The core component of civilization is empathy (Warmoth). All the great world religions recommend the Golden Rule as the central wisdom of their faith and the core human understanding to getting along. That is the Generalized Other. It is a recognition of our common humanity.

Mead thought of it as a political strategy for transforming the world. We have buried Mead's true intention and meaning just like we buried David Hume's. Hume did not stop by demolishing the philosophical foundation of scientific and showing that an inductive science would not reveal how to live. He then proceeded to write what he considered his master work saying "sympathy" must be the basis for our knowledge about how to live together. Mead and Hume's vision reminds of today's restorative justice circles. Hal Pepinsky suggests the process of democracy (taking others into account) is just such a responsive dynamic and its opposite is violence (refusing to take others into account).

Mead's is an evolutionary theory of human consciousness. Mead maintained universal community was the ideal of history—the ideal towards which humans had always aspired. This is not a theory but a force that can be observed at work in history (Cronk). Mead saw three movements towards the ideal of universal community—the "ultimate values toward which creation moved" (Mead, 1938: 504) The first is the common dream of most religions—the family of humanity based on love. The second—economic exchange—moves rapidly beyond boundaries to establish contact but produces mainly superficial relationships. The third is communication. Notice Mead's is not a finished model but allows room for the human. As he says, "It indicates direction, not destination" (Mead, 1938: 519). Communication must always be an ongoing process. It is the key.

> The human social ideal—the ideal or ultimate goal of human social progress—is the attainment of a universal human society in which all human individuals would possess a perfected social intelligence, such that . . . the meanings of any one individual's acts or gestures . . . would be the same for any other individual whatever who responded to them. (Mead, 1934: 310)

In other words, when someone said or did something, everyone in the world would know what they meant. We might not agree or like it, but we would understand. Someone might even fly an airplane into the World Trade Center, and people would understand what they were saying.

From Tribe to Humanity

The movement of evolution must move beyond self, family, tribe, nation to embrace all of humanity. As Bergson noted, we will never get to a kinship with all humanity by simply expanding the in-group outwards—it is always by a leap of intuition that we sense our common humanity (Bergson, 1935: 267). Erich Fromm wrote love which simply expands outward to include your family, club or team is simply an enlarged selfishness.

It is normal to become very attached to those who are familiar to us. We root for the home team. But there is no need to give this any biological hocus pocus. Establishing what is "me" and what is "not me" is a fundamental social process. A unified Science of Humanity would work to understand elementary human processes. We tend to create "in-groups" and "out-groups." Comedian Dick Gregory once noted, humans of all races on earth would achieve instant equality and harmony if we were only invaded by creatures from outer space. Having a common enemy can give us an identity. Jung showed how we often deny our own faults, project them onto others and attempt to eliminate them over there. Scapegoating is a natural social psychological mechanism for denial. However, in an age of nuclear, chemical and biological weapons, fundamental worldviews which see the foreign other as the source of all evil are a threat to human survival. As Jung showed, psychological health involves learning to own and deal with our faults rather than projecting them onto others.

In-group – out-group is a social tendency but it is not inevitable. We tend to identify with those like us and fear those who are different. It is the most common factor research shows related to racial prejudice. Counterbalancing this process historically is the ideal of love: "if we say that it embraces all humanity; we should not be going too far, we should hardly be going far enough, since its love may extend to animals, to plants, to all nature" (Bergson, 1935, p. 38).

Classical economic and political theories posit the idea of separate individuals. They fail to appreciate how we are also intertwined. The very definition of social interaction is "mutual influence." People who interact take the other into account shifting their actions in anticipation of reactions. Conservatives have an unrealistic all or nothing approach to self and society. They bounce back and forth between viewing individuals as totally independent or demanding they conform to group authority. They never develop an accurate understanding. Sociobiology also embraces this same absurdity. The truth is more complicated. Self and Community are interdependent. We need to get the "we" conversation right. Society is not just a bunch of separated individuals.

Power—Self Love, Selfishness, and Community

Sociobiology talks about the individual as if the social does not exist. Today's sociobiology embraces the theories of history's most extreme champion of rugged individualism—Herbert Spencer. They suggest individuals are innately selfish but that what they call the core evolutionary process—the wisdom of the market—works for a higher good. Spencer coined the phrase "survival of the fittest" to justify social inequality. It is the ultimate conservativism. It is circular to say "survival of the fittest" because whatever survives can be argued to have been best fitted to survive. It is like saying, whatever is, is.

Spencer thought Nature alone drove social evolution, and humans are powerless to change it. To Spencer society was no more than a collection of individuals. In a letter to Lester Ward (1918, III, 213, Spencer wrote he would "regard social progress as mainly a question of character . . . The inherited . . . natures of individuals, only little modifiable . . . ." Spencer was himself isolated—a rich, lonely man whose last twenty years were spent with illness and drugs. He would conclude: "If pessimism means that you would rather not have lived, then I am a pessimist."

Sociobiologists do not understand selfishness is not an effective path to self esteem. Realistic self fulfillment can best be achieved in the context of community. As Kant noted, the social ideal towards which we should strive is "maximum individuality within maximum community."

Sociobiologists do not understand power and the interrelationship between self and other. The early behavioral scientists worked to discover the core social and psychological processes. The child must successfully learn to balance its own needs with the desires of others. Freud calls this the anal phase. This is no mere illustration. It is the genius of Freud that he locates the dilemma exactly where it is—in the bodily needs. You don't have all the power. You can't always do what you want because there are other people in the world and their desires intrude. However, you can't give your power away completely to please others because your are living and also have needs. Toilet training is the exact process whereby the child learns to balance the conflict between its own needs and the demands of others. The child may repress and postpone to accommodate the outside world but eventually when you've got to go, you've got to go. The lesson of all psychology is that if needs are repressed in one form, they resurface in another. We can either honestly address our needs or end up playing interpersonal games that fools others and perhaps ourselves. Either way, needs will out.

As a student of Freud's Alfred Adler articulated, power between parent and child is further complicated by the fact that the small child is powerless to oppose the will of more powerful adults. To achieve a feeling of well being, the child must somehow manage to compensate for this inferiority. Parents want to assert their own wishes but also want to raise a well adjusted child. How do you influence a child without destroying feelings of self worth? In an unhealthy resolution of this dilemma, the children overcompensates feeling they must put others down in order to feel good about themselves.

The successful staging of self esteem must be win-win—"I'm O.K., You're O.K." to use the language of transactional analysis. As etiquette understands, a successful social interaction demands both people are able to walk away feeling good about themselves. The unhealthy ways of resolving the conflict between self and other are where I repress my needs for your convenience (You're O.K., I'm not O.K.) or I trample on you to get my needs met (I'm O.K., you're not O.K.).

Self fulfillment takes place in the context of community. Fromm shows in *The Art of Loving,* self love and selfishness are actually opposites. Love is the same whether it is directed towards ourselves or others. Maslow's research showed self actualized people are able to drop their boundaries and allow others in. It is people who don't love themselves who must cling to ego like it was pure gold. The attitudes we have towards ourselves tend to be the same as our attitudes towards others. Buber says the word "I" always is contained in a word pair of either "I–Thou" or "I–It." If we treat others as objects, we are likely to treat ourselves as an object. If we treat ourselves with respect and caring to our needs, we are apt to treat others as also a "Thou."

Sociobiology makes the same mistake as economic exchange theory. It sees individuals as separate entities who exchange interpersonal commodities back and forth across rigid boundaries. Other people are objects to be used and seen in terms of what they can bring in benefits to self. This is an "I–It" relationship. However, people also form relationships where identities merge and Other is seen as an important part of self. I love you and my significance depends on you also being alright.

Sociobiologists cite the statistics showing stepchildren are 100 times more likely to be abused than biological children (Daly and Wilson 1998:28). They say there must be something biological for the relationship to be that great. Why? For the natural parent, children are defined as part of "Me." Stepchildren are "Not-Me" and any inclusion is more artificial. It is easier to be define stepchildren as objects—even sexual objects. It is easier to cross a line of social convention (and loyalty to the mother) than with a daughter conceived of as your own flesh and blood. Biological parents also watched the child grow from an infant while the stepfather often arrived on the scene late. Incest is one of our strongest social taboos although cultures define it differently. It is a commitment not to treat some people as objects. We incorporate others as part of our identity. There does not have to be anything genetic about it.

We are one. And we are two. That is pretty fundamental, but it is where we must start. Individuation sketches the process by which we become separate individuals. Power deals with the conflict between competing needs and agendas and how people feel good about themselves. How do we come together in a relationship or as a community and still retain our individuality?

Love–The Life Force

Without love and human contact, children do not grow normally and often die or are developmentally disabled. Human beings testify love is the most important part of life. However, love is one of those secret springs objective science ignored and stuffed into the right side of the brain. It is hard to find a way to talk about love and be taken seriously in scientific circles.

We would have a quite different view of evolutionary forces with love at the core. And with all apologies to objective scientists, that is exactly where humanists would place it. You want a sociobiology? Start with love. There is no better place to start. Love is basic to the human organism.

Sociobiologists say love is only an emotion and like legislation and sausage, we don't want to see how feelings are made (Pinker, 2002). Is love just a feeling inside the brain based on a chemical process? Is love just a by-product? Martin Buber (1970: 66) was most insistent love is not a feeling. Buber conceives of love as a real spirit between people.

> Feelings accompany . . . love, but they do not constitute it. . . . Feelings one 'has'; love occurs. . . . This is no metaphor but actuality: love . . . is between I and You. Whoever does not know this, know this with his being, does not know love . . . . (Buber, 1970: 66).

Love is a fundamental drive for union at the core of existence. We could call it the desire for connection, overcoming separateness or a primal urge. Sociobiologists would call it the need for "genetic closeness." However, I don't see how that improves our understanding.

If we are going to forge an agreement between sociobiology and the behavioral sciences, what is important is to recognize love as core process. Merely calling it genetic and quickly moving off misses the deep understandings of psychology. Sociobiology would want to simplify this as a chemical process based on genetic replicators. But such mechanistic reductionism misses a great deal.

> no serious student of man would want to exchange the richness of our understanding of man gained from fields like psychoanalysis and social psychology for the one we get from zoology (even broadly considered). Admittedly it is basic, graphic, sometimes even humorous, warm, and poetic—but it is thin. A whole book on flocking behavior does not give us the depth and complexity of a single page on group dynamics; a whole shelf on the vicious of animal aggression, or even on the inhibitors of it, does not convey the subtlety of a single page on human scapegoating, on the psychology of buying off one's own death, one page of Erwin Strauss on the dynamics of miserliness is worth a volume on primate selfishness. (Becker, 1974: 249)

It is important is that we linger here. The point of psychology is that *people do get attached—and moving off is not so easily done.* A child's first emotional bond has deep implications. Breaking away from parents and establishing identity as a separate life is complicated. Neither will ever be completely independent. Parent and child carry each other inside as long as either shall live. There can never be an all or nothing resolution. Their feelings are interdependent. Erich Fromm translates Freud's wayward Oedipal metaphor into existential terms. How things are resolved between parent and child influence how we learn to form intimate bonds with others. The existential dilemma of love is how to bond without consuming or being consumed.

Freud said there is a life force—what he called the libido. Fromm says Freud did not understand sex deeply enough. Fromm sees sex as part of the primal desire for union. Let us remember mother and child once were one. All energy isn't sexual energy. The human animal must find a way of overcoming separateness and feeling at home in the universe. There is no need to see achieving union with your parents by conforming to their wishes or even creative activity as sublimated sex drive. Sex is one way of overcoming separateness and achieving union but it is not the only way. Fromm (1956) notes other ways to overcome separateness include conformity, orgiastic feasts of sex or food, giving your life to the Fatherland, creative activity. Fromm says the only satisfactory answer to the problem of existence is love which he defines as "fusion under conditions of integrity." It is a win-win situation where neither person is sacrificed for the sake of relationship.

There are many ways to achieve union and overcome separateness. Freud had posited both a life force and a death force. Denis de Rougemont does a content analysis of literature in *Love in the Western World*. The lover and the soldier share much the same fate. Passion seeks to obliterate separateness by merging with the cosmos in some grand destiny. Much of what passes for romance is almost like a love affair with death seeking mystic annihilation of self. Such romance does not work because it is a "twin narcissism." The other is needed only so as to unleash a script in order to feel aflame and not loved as th e real person he or she really is.

> passion, born of a fatal desire for mystical union, may be regarded as open to being surpassed and fulfilled only thanks to the meeting with some other, and the admission of this other's alien life and ever distinct person, which although distinct, holds the promise of unending alliance and begins a real dialog.
>
> Then dread having been banished by response and nostalgia by presence, we both cease . . . to suffer, and accept our daylight. (De Rougemont, 1956, pp. 322–323).

True love requires two full selves. That take mature people who have learned how to balance self and other. And that is a difficult lesson.

> Love is the drive for reunion of the separated. It presupposes that there is something to be reunited, something relatively independent that stands upon itself. . . . Without this justice there is no reunitive love, because there is nothing to unite (Tillich, 1954, pp. 68-69).

There are two core processes at the core of creation -- the desire for oneness (overcoming separateness and feeling at home in the universe) and the desire for differentiation (separateness, identity). What do we do about others? What do we do about society?

Authoritarianism, Conformity, Democracy

> A good deal of research in sociobiology indicates that humans have been built by evolution to prefer authoritarian forms of government—that is parent-like leadership as opposed to a democratic form of government.
>
> —Tom Arcaro and Chrissy Kilgariff, 2003

Hiding behind rote biological determinism to give up on democracy is dangerous. The necessity of authoritarianism is a severe misreading.

Much of psychology has dealt with the parent-child bond. Freud would even eventually say the Oedipus complex really was about the relationship of the child to both parents. The child learns to quell existential anxiety by obedience to parental wishes but at the cost of denying its own feelings. It is a costly bargain Alice Miller (1983) calls the poisonous pedagogy. The child can't just go back to marry the parents' reality and live happily ever after.

Conforming to authority is also social in nature. It is a flight from existential insecurity as Fromm shows in *Escape from Freedom* that is his analysis of fascism and authoritarianism. Democracy is a social invention. Many cultures don't have a tradition of democracy. Even in America, we don't seem to understand democracy is something you do and not just a logo. That makes it hard to export. C. Wright Mills maintained the idea of democracy is a strange paradox—a group that supports the ideal of individuality. All the social research on conformity shows a tendency for groups to stamp out individuality. There is security in going along with the crowd or conforming to authority rather than having to stand out as an individual. Most people do not stand up to authority or to the group—although it is important to note research shows a significant small percent do.

We might say democracy is not in our natures but more correctly, it is a natural to want to get your own way. When we are in power it is tempting to neglect the rights of those who disagree with us. Democracy is an ideal. It is a dialogue born of enlightened self interest—it could have been me. There are no guarantees. We must constantly remind ourselves of the ideal—to respect people and to take others into account. It is the belief that healthy conflict and respecting the needs of all will produce the best society. It is easy when you are top dog to exploit others. In times of danger, fascists argue they will keep us safe. In economic scarcity, there is not enough to go around so the powerful are even more likely to want to horde and keep others down. It's easy to believe your own group is capable of self government but the lower class (or third world people) are not. It is always hard to balance the rights of winners and the needs of losers.

It is true many leaders have chosen to treat their people like children. However, there is no biological necessity for conformity or authoritarian structures.

Sociobiologists still suggest society must be a Big Parent repressing animal urges and keeping people under control. It is the voice of Freud. But we must go deeper.

> [we need to] get at both the basic animality and the larger ontological and phenomenological problems that are missed by a simple instinctual reductionism—just as Freud himself missed them. The 'monsters' that are unleashed from the id are not primal drives from the dim recesses of racial memory. They are forces of hate and destruction that struggle against the insignificance of the creature, and that will take their toll to overcome that insignificance. (Becker, 1974: 243)

Many sociobiologists insist the human animal is naturally aggressive and any exceptions merely show the power of culture—that it can even manages to repress our true biological nature. It is a no-win argument. A more correct way to talk is that there are core existential (or animal) needs, which can be met in very different ways. As Becker notes in *Escape from Evil*:

> it is one thing to say man . . . is a vicious animal, and another to say that it is because he is a frightened creature who tries to secure a victory over his limitations . . . it is the disguise of panic that makes men live in ugliness and not the natural animal wallowing. . . . this means that evil itself is now amenable to critical analysis and, conceivably, to the sway of reason. (1975: 169)

It is true that with the step from hunting and gathering societies and simple horticultural societies to the late agrarian and industrial societies that human evil has become a larger problem. But that does not mean we are doomed to increasing evil. Knowledge might be turned to understanding human problems and creating human betterment.

Notes

1. The evidence that people are hungry for a relevant theory that puts everything together abounds: increasing alienation, the growth of simplest, holistic explanations and fundamentalism. People need as Erich Fromm says, a framework of orientation—a way of making sense of the universe. As secular science advanced, it yielded technological marvels but left meaning more problematic. People are searching for comprehensive answers.

2. Liberals believe in relativism. They are skeptical and afraid of the true believer and putting values on others. Conservatives understand we can't keep values out of the endeavor. Liberals acknowledge that values influence methodology but still wish it were not so and strive towards value neutrality.

3. Some argue: "your genes do not care if you are happy or not, just that they get passed on to another generation. We are not designed for maximum happiness, but maximum survival." (Arcaro and Kilgariff, 2003) I must disagree. Organisms seek a basic subjective feeling of well being. Even many medical doctors will tell you, happiness makes a difference.

A leading sociobiology book is called *The Selfish Gene*. However, genes are not selfish. Having deplored anthropomorphizing culture, it makes no sense to turn around and anthropomorphize genes. Genes are little mechanical replicators borrowed from a mechanistic worldview. Genes don't have a survival instinct. It is a process. Like sediment being laid down to form mountains, it just sort of happens. To characterize human beings as being concerned with self interest makes sense. Calling something the selfish gene takes us off on the tangents of conservative economic and political theories.

4. As Charles Hampden-Turner (1970) shows in "The Borrowed Toolbox and Conservative Man," the scientific method is conservative. It is biased towards "what is" rather than "what could be"/"should be." It embraces detachment. It emphasizes *controlling*—knowledge based on prediction and control naturally lends itself to manipulation—such is inherent in the method. A method of suspicion, testing and doubt produces a quite different world-view than trust and the willing suspension of disbelief might reveal. The scientific doesn't have direction built in—value-free knowledge that can be used for fair or foul by whatever "powers that be" who have the most money to purchase it.

Chapter 8:

Progressive Politics:

The Mind Intervenes in Evolution

Taking Life in Our Hands

The Social Gospel Movement from the 1870s into the early twentieth century was a very different version of evolution than Spencer's laissez faire rugged individualism. The early American sociologists were predominately ministers who felt the human calling is to alleviate as much human suffering as can be done by human hands and move us as close to heaven on earth as possible.

Most early sociologists from Comte on believed in Human Progress at least as much as they believed in Science. Their version of progress was a different version from predestination or manifest destiny. They believed human intelligence had evolved to the point that it should now be turned to the task of making a better society.

In Europe, Karl Marx's ideas about intervening in human history for human betterment attracted a following and would lead to the Communist revolution. His famous line was: "The philosophers have described the world. It is now up to us to transform it." The Great Depression in America led to social reforms aimed to improve life. When perpetual Socialist candidate for president Norman Thomas was asked what happened to socialism in America, he would say FDR watered it down and passed it.

Many sociobiologists now claim the failure of communism in the Soviet Union and waning of the welfare state demonstrate the folly of social experiments and any intervention into human affairs. Sociobiologists suggest conservatives understand the wisdom of the system—the free market—whereas liberals need to manage everything. Such reminds me of Albion Small's comment that the longer we refuse to acknowledge Marx's insights, the longer will his fame and reputation grow.

Conflict produces benefits but it also produces abuses. The rich and powerful don't really believe in free markets—that's just a marquee. They want the public to not peek while they manipulate government behind the scenes for their own benefits. Free enterprise isn't free. We make huge investments in the playing field and the shape of the game. As economist Peter Drucker once said, in the United States, we have "socialism for the rich and rugged individualism for the poor."

Society involves both social processes and human made social constructions. A realistic conversation would be about when we can rely on the pursuit of self interest and how does it let us down? One can certainly find examples of social interventions which made matters worse. However, that doesn't mean humans must throw up their hands as the Social Darwinists would have it and let whatever happens happen. The great God of the economic system should not be plunder and greed. There is a difference between self interest and selfishness. Thomas Jefferson worried about the fate of the young American democracy fearing the monied interests might rig the game and destroy equal opportunity for others. Power should not make right. We should follow the research on dealing with school yard bullies and as a group delegitimize greed. We certainly should not design a system that rewards it.

Sociobiologists are reviving all the old stables of exchange theory—Homans, the principle of least interest, the Prisoner's Dilemma, arguments against the possibility of altruism. But economic selfishness disguised as biology does not make the best world. The only way to win the Prisoner's Dilemma is to recognize we have mutual interests in the meta-game. However, the conservative worldview

> looks to the past instead of facing forward, regards man in the light of animals and fails to respect his complexity. Their 'games' which simulate life view it as a competitive struggle for scarce resources, rather than the synergistic creation of abundance. (Hampden Turner, 1970)

Actually conservatives don't even take our animal needs seriously. Ending world hunger isn't charity. If a bunch of greedy human animals horde to increase their power, their wealth and their status while other human animals don't have food and clean water, then we are asking for wars and terrorism. We are going to have to find better ways to satisfy the human needs for status and power as well as for food and clean water.

Sociobiologists embrace primitive concepts of classic economic theory and old style political science which view human beings as primarily motivated by money and force. However, behavioral science has developed a much more comprehensive picture over the past century. Even an extensive body of research by B. F. Skinner showed rewards are more effective than punishments for animals. For the human animal, intelligence makes the attraction of pulls even more important. Maslow showed meaning is motivation and for the human animal, rewards (the pulls of "being" motivators, e.g. love & meaning) represent a different realm than punishments, i.e. "deficiency" motivators (the pushes of hunger, pain, fear, exposure to the elements, insecurity). There is a direction to evolution. Human desires and purposes intrude. As Lester Ward and most sociologists of his day understood, the social forces are human needs and purposes. Human beings want better (however they might define it) and a sense of personal well being.

For all their talk about a new kind of Republican, today's conservatives represent the policies of Calvin Coolidge and Herbert Hoover. Their arguments and theories are the same as the industrialists and Social Darwinists of the late nineteenth and early twentieth century. Today's sociobiologists also are trotting out these old theories. We are back to the founding arguments of the discipline.

Should sociology even exist? Does it have anything important to contribute? What is wrong with a rugged individualism that relies on the evolutionary force of the market to take care of all social needs? What can be changed by human intervention and by human reason? Should government intervene in human affairs to improve human welfare?

A Science of Humanity Awaits

Please do not miss the point: social science originated to be a conscious force in human evolution. No wonder sociobiologists whose paradigm bias is conservative (detached, uninvolved observation of what is) would be anxious to declare such a view dead. Both the sociobiologists' and the conservatives' best friends—the "powers that be"—promote the wisdom of a laissez faire approach to society.

But sociology was not supposed to be hands off. Sociology was supposed to be hands on. That is why sociobiologists are so intent upon destroying the left wing focus of sociology and leaving only a dead remnant of the discipline to serve the needs of the masters.

We can see today deep into the genetic structure as just a few decades ago we could split the atom at its core. But we have made no moral progress. Conservative theories threaten to turn the world into an eternal war. "See, we told you so," they say, "human beings are evil." In his biography of Lester Ward who originated the term applied sociology, Samuel Chugerman wrote:

> One of the obvious facts in social evolution is the persistence of social problems in spite of all progress flowing from inventions and discoveries which were directly intended to solve such problems . . . moral progress has been negligible. The explanation of this paradox is not found in evil human nature, but in the lack of applied social science, and the stubborn resistance of even so-called moral elements in society to any basic improvements in the condition of the mass.

To repeat the quote used in the Introduction to this book, "Instead of preaching morality in the midst of an immoral social system of dog eat dog, . . . Ward argues for an entirely new concept of ethics based upon an intelligent, planned social order in which the principle of 'every man for himself' . . . will not exist." (Chugerman, 1939: pp. 547–549)

Remember Ward was active in the late 1800s. The same struggles being fought out then in the United States are being repeated today only now they've gone global. Ironically, the battlegrounds are the same industries—Big Oil, the banking industry, the garment industry. Can unleashed capitalism answer all human needs? Are free markets the answer? Or should as Ward argued, we give "more attention to the problem of happiness and less to that of amassing wealth.[so that] moral progress will have a chance." (Chugerman, 1939: pp. 547–549)

The goal of social evolution, as conceived by the early American sociologists, was moral progress. Applied sociology would lead. Moral progress only occurs when the human animal takes life in our own hands and decides to act on the knowledge intellect provides. Then and only then, will we have a Science of Humanity.

Technology Will Not Save Us

The machines we build, being artificial organs that are added to our natural organs, extend their scope, and thus enlarge the body of humanity. If that body is to be kept entire and its movements regulated, the soul must expand in turn; otherwise its equilibrium will be threatened and grave difficulties will arise...between the soul of mankind, hardly changed from its original state, and its enormously enlarged body.

—Henri Bergson's 1927 Nobel Prize acceptance speech

Ogburn and Nimkoff would adopt a detached, scientific view of this thing saying social culture inevitably lags behind technology. It's just the way it is. This is the ultimate conservative doctrine. Ogburn in his 1929 ASA presidential address would say, "sociology is not interested in making the world a better place."

The early sociologists thought that culture must lead. Technology without moral progress can only take us so far. As we look down at earth's body as we ride high above in our airliners; as we count the collateral damage from our "smart" bombs; as we clean up the pollution of unanticipated consequences, we must seek solutions that count the cost.

The human intellect has evolved to invent vast technological resources which can script our own destruction: biological, chemical and nuclear weapons, pollution possibilities to end life on the planet, genetically modified food, human cloning. We must literally take human life and the planet in our hands. Evolve or die. And we do not have time to wait for genetic mutations. The next step in human evolution will be conscious or not at all.

Biology is Not Destiny

As feminists said so clearly: Biology is not destiny. In 1964, birth control pills separated women from the inevitability of childbirth and spawned a sexual and cultural revolution. The Catholic Church was immediately up in arms about interfering with nature but even its own laity paid only slight attention to the advice of celibate priests.

Abortion was a different matter. It has become one of the crucial battle lines of our time. Who defines human life? We know the embryo goes through all the stages of evolution while in the womb. It does not develop the advanced brain anthropologists associate with the step to humankind until after the sixth month. Is it a child or a fertilized egg?

Even though we can see down to the molecular level, who gets to decide whether to convey human status on this fertilized egg? Trotting out arguments from religious authorities doesn't help. We are back to Martin Luther nailing a document on the church door. You and your God have to decide where to draw the line. Feminists say this should be a basic human right—to be able to have control over your own body and make the choice with your God and your conscience. Experts can't decide the ultimate questions of life. There is no great scientific Authority who can tell us. Science fails us in the ultimate questions of life. It is a mystery. What happens after death is a matter of faith. And no one knows for sure what happens before birth.

Abortion is only the tip of an iceberg. Human cloning looms on the horizon. Fetal tissue research stood to alleviate the suffering of even conservative ex-President Ronald Reagan and we found his wife campaigning for it. Love does take us past ideological boundaries. What is important? What matters? What lines do we draw and where?

As public opinion expert Daniel Yankelovich (1991) says, democracy depends upon realizing we can't rely on authorities for the crucial decisions—experts can tell us how to make a nuclear bomb but they cannot tell us whether it should be done. The values must be ours. Is a nuclear bomb for oil profits worth the price? How about a nuclear power plant in my neighborhood? Do genetically modified foods increase our profits or our risk of cancer? And what about this strange disease called cancer? Is it just because we are living longer? Or are we altering the earth's body and our habitat in ways that cause our own bodies to mutate cancerous cells?

With technology unleashed, when do we take responsibility—aware of the interconnectedness of all things? We do not act with impunity no matter how strong we think we are. For every action, there is a reaction. Terrorism should teach us that. With the advance of technology, individuals may soon have their own personal nuclear devices, biological and chemical weapons just like we today have personal computers.

We can no longer continue to separate mind from matter, mind from politics, and technology from a conversation about what matters. George W. Bush has the greatest arsenal of any superman in history and a third grade cartoon-show understanding of human behavior. We cannot let technology lead. We must make values matter.

Like a modern day Frankenstein monster, a conversation at the top of the world awaits. An unconscious, value-free technology will not take us where we want to go. What have we unleashed and what would we make?

Decisions Once Reserved for Gods

It is getting frightfully late in human history for the ostrich approach known as today's conservatism. In the nineteenth century, we saw Herbert Spencer "despite his extreme libertarianism, regard society as the machine of the gods which can only be described but not controlled" (Chugerman, 1939: 305). Conservatives want to just leave God alone. The universe is a big machine set up by God, let it be. Bow down before the ultimate authority—of God and Nature. There is no room for human involvement. Turn off your intellect and have faith.

When Spinoza reached the "God or Nature" conclusion, religion and values went one way and science another. But it didn't have to be that way. We could have instead dumped the metaphor of the universe as a machine with a mechanical God pulling the levers (or driven by genetic replicators). We could have instead entered into a dialogue with God and the infinite. It is the ultimate conversation about values. How shall we shape the universe? In what direction do we move creation?

With human hands and a valueless technology, we have made some dreadful things. But what if we would not separate values from world? What sort of world should we design?

Conservatives say respect authority—we have the truth. But you see, that's just the problem. They don't have the truth. What they create depends upon where they start. That brings us back to the ultimate conversation: in which values should we place our faith?

Reducing all of life to mechanical chemical replicators such as genes destroys much of what we know as humans. Saying this does not mean we deny our animal heritage. What it does is question the wisdom of insisting on the mechanical metaphor for science.

The twentieth century "God is Dead" movement was really about the death of a mechanical God and the emergence of a new way of being and knowing life (and God if you will). Sociobiology would struggle to get all this back in the mechanistic framework of science as if it never happened. But we must push the dialog to a New Being and a new relationship with the infinite. It is a mature relationship of a child grown up from the cave. It is Bergson's dialog between creature and creator. It is an adult relationship with God (or life). How do we shape the human?

Sociobiology is revisiting all the classic arguments. One stop is B.F. Skinner's *Beyond Freedom and Dignity*. Skinner argues that like it or not, we have vast powers and people are going to be manipulated. He says we need to surrender outmoded ideals such as freedom and human dignity. I could not disagree more. Some things are sacred. There are limits beyond which we must not go—limits beyond which we cannot go without destroying the human.

> It may sound strange, but perhaps we must discuss the theology of our brand of sociology. Theologians would claim that a loving God allows free will and therefore does not control the outcome. A loving God values the human. A loving social science must do the same. A humanistic social science cannot opt for prediction and control that destroys free will and the human. (Du Bois and Wright, 2002)

As Becker (1968, p. 364) notes, "opting for man as an end, . . . means introducing indeterminacy into the world." That is what it means to be a humanist. If we are to allow free will, we can't control the outcome. We must have faith in people. Parents know that. Real lovers know that. Why don't politicians, managers and scientists know that? You can't have it both ways, you either have free will or not. If children always do as their parents want, then their freedom is untested and only hypothetical.

We need to control say the conservatives. "We will keep you safe." Fear brings that strategy. But authoritarian strategies never work. There are never enough troops or surveillance and prisons. Do you really believe our bombs and missiles and surveillance are fail safe?

The spirit of humanity is sacred. Is the Golden Rule practical? Should we trade in freedom for security? Where do we put our faith? We must somehow find a way to live together and share a world.

What We've Learned So Far

As Ernest Becker (1974) says, sociobiology is "speaking the truth falsely." Human beings are not a blank slate. That is absolutely right. There are limits to human nature. True. But as Fromm notes, it is not that we cannot twist humanity in convoluted way — it is that there are terrible consequences when we violate human nature. The human tries to get out no matter in what twisted warped way it must struggle to poke its little head out of the confines.

Rather than starting fresh with a sociobiology that knows little about behavioral science, let's ask what have we learned about human nature in 150 years of sociology and psychology. In *The Structure of Evil*, Becker concludes what social science has learned about evil is this:

[It] showed exactly what Comte had wanted: the fullest possible correlates of the dependence of personal troubles on social issues.

The problem for all thinkers of the Enlightenment, and especially for Comte, was how to get social interest to predominate over selfish private interest. The new theory of alienation showed ethical action could not be possible where man was not supplied with self critical and socially critical knowledge, and with the possibilities of broad and responsible choices. Recurrent evils like sadism, militant hate, competitive greed, narrow-pride, calculating self-interest that takes a non-chalant view of others' lives. . . all stem from constrictions on behavior and from shallowness of meanings; and these could be lap in the lap of society. . . and the kinds of choices and cognition which its institutions encourage and permit. Man could only be ethical if he was strong, and he could only be strong if he was given fullest possible cognition, and responsible control over his own powers. The only possible ethics was one which took man as a center, and which provided him with the conditions that permitted him to try to be moral.

The antidote to evil was not to impose a crushing sense of supernatural sanction, or unthinking obligation or automatic beliefs of any kind—no matter how 'cheerful' they seem. For the first time in history it had become transparently clear that the real antidote to evil in society was to supply the possibility of depth and wholeness or experience. . . . It had never been so well understood that goodness and human nature were potentially synonymous terms; and evil was a complex reflex of the coercion of human powers (Non-inclusive language original) (1968, pp. 325–326)

We are not just the creature trapped in the maze. We can choose to look up, see the environments which shape our behaviors, and change the environments. The core design principle must be to start with our understanding of what it means to be human. We can only violate it at a terrible cost.

While B.F. Skinner is very wrong about freedom and dignity, he is right about the other half of his argument. Human beings have come through the looking glass and there is no going back. It is not a matter of whether to shape the world or not. Our only choice is whether to do it consciously with attention to what we want or to just allow it happen by chance. Human intellect won't go away. We have the power. If we abstain, we are just giving the decision to others. The Enrons, military powers and Big Oil companies are very much trying to shape the world and human destiny. We enter that crucial conversation which makes us tremble to our core.

North Dakota has the lowest repeat rate for juvenile offenders in the nation. They hire an independent Colorado firm to track real numbers not just what looks good. They have a 10% repeat rate. The next lowest state has 30% rate. Most are 40–50% ranging all the way up to 70%. As Eastern North Dakota Director of Juvenile Corrections Lisa Bjergaard says, it all begins with a philosophy. They start by asking what kind of person they want at the end. It is the question for all social designers.

The Politics of Biology—Conservatives and Liberals, the Body and the Ideal

No where is the bias of today's crop of sociobiologists more pronounced than with politics. Conservative interpretations of history, politics and economics are being projected onto biology. In what pretends to be *A Darwinian Left,* Peter Singer concludes his book by saying we need "a sharply deflated vision of the left, its utopian dreams replaced by a coolly realistic view of what can be achieved." With such a version of the left, we scarcely need conservatives.

Who gets to decide what is realistic? Sociologists and human beings must contend against such views. Much of Sociobiology stems from sophomoric versions psychology and sociology and misunderstanding of basics such as the difference between self love and. selfishness, alternatives to exchange theory, the relationship between self and community, and how to effectively manage and motivate people.

Many sociologists and psychologists seem not to understand the pronouncements of sociobiologists are just that—pronouncements. We must not be enamored by the hard sciences and give them too much weight. We should realize:

> The world has been created by two conflicting tendencies. One of them represents matter which, in its own consciousness, tends downwards; the second is life with its innate sentiment of freedom and its perpetually creative force, which tends increasingly toward the light of knowledge and limitless horizons.
> —Per Hallstrom, remarks presenting Nobel Prize to Henri Bergson, 1927

Mind heads for the horizon—the ideal world. And body is stuck here on the ground. The mind-body split undoubtedly originated in the human animal's desire to separate spirit from a body it knew would die.

Biologist Konrad Lorenz attacked the lack of humility of an animal creature who is a product of evolution but sees itself as made in the image of God. Sociobiologists note we cannot so quickly abandon our bodies and head to pure spirit. And yet in their haste to reduce all of life to a mechanical objectivity, sociobiologists also can't be accused of humility (Becker, 1974). Their grand pronouncements claim knowledge of all of life and implications for what is possible and impossible for human culture.

We must not so quickly abandon the ideals which have filled the human heart across time and history. As Becker (1968) notes, the science of man is utopian in its very nature. We must have a vision of the ideal if we are to move in that direction. Utopia is not a destination. It is a direction. But between mind from body, between the real and the ideal, there is a world to make.

Human nature surely provides parameters. But we must be careful to not ground the human potential in someone's mistaken version of a biological imperative. Grounded in what we know of life, what can we actually say is impossible for the human animal?

War on the Human Potential

There is nothing that sends sociobiologists and conservatives on a rampage faster than Jose Ortega y Gasset's (1941: 200) statement: "Man is no thing, but a drama. . . . Man, in a word, has no nature; what he has is . . . history." (Ellipsis Original)

In his book *Blank Slate: The Modern Denial of Human Nature*, sociobiologist Steven Pinker (2002) rants at this as the cornerstone of the modern denial of human nature. He sees it as the liberal "denial of imperfectability." Rejected Supreme Court nominee Robert Bork (1996), who remains a darling of ultraconservatives, heads straight for denouncing the same quote in *Slouching Towards Gomorrah: Modern Liberalism and American Decline*. He ridicules both the human potential movement and the counterculture. Conservatives want to eliminate any notion that human nature is a self fulfilling prophecy. They want to close that chapter in human history completely.

Modern science was born in the seventeenth and eighteenth century Enlightenment idea that human reason could be used to improve conditions, life, and happiness. The mind-body split went off in different directions. Physical sciences set out to discover the real world of matter—rocks and bodies and things. Treating the world as an object, would lead to all sorts of technological breakthroughs. The other direction didn't look like a science at all. The human mind went straight towards the horizon—human affairs and the perfectibility of man. It is an important part of our story, because those folks led to American Revolution and the French Revolution. As Ernest Becker (1971) outlines, it was only when these revolutionary movements got blocked and became routinized, that revolutionary dreamers came indoors to regroup and build a science of humanity.

It was also at this time in the 1800s, that the physical sciences who were enjoying great success with technological breakthroughs and public adulation turned their eye towards mind. However, with the split of mind from matter, we had separated values from action. When the focus of the physical sciences turned to mind, science couldn't change methods without calling off the whole charade of objectivity. So we focused on building theories to explain other people but not quite big enough to understand the hand of life or even ourselves. We could manipulate and control, but we did not understand. And from this convoluted lenses, our new knowledge of biology and genetics emerges.

Pinker's (2002) characterization is that when Wilson first wrote *Sociobiology*, he stumbled innocently into political controversy. As he tells the story, the poor fellow was just trying to be objective. But you see that's the problem. We can't have a world without values. The human animal must prioritize in order to make decisions and live. Human nature is the ultimate political and religious battleground. The pretense of objectivity will not do. Remember it was Wilson who said of Marx, "wonderful theory, wrong species." (And he thought that was just objective?)

Sociobiologists would say humans can't be changed but scientists have no trouble changing the world—cloning, genetically altered foods, pesticides, chemical and biological weapons, nuclear weapons, the biosphere—those things can be changed. Moral progress however, they claim is not possible. This is just the way humans are. But there are other alternatives. However if we are to move in a direction, we would have to pick up values.

Sociobiologists claim they are scientists who are being objective. As Steven Pinker (2001: 422) writes: "Acknowledging human nature does not mean overturning our personal world views, and I would have nothing to suggest as a replacement if it did. It means only taking intellectual life out of its parallel universe and reuniting it with science . . ."

It could not be said better. It is the summary of both what is right and what is wrong about sociobiology. Pinker is right that we need to acknowledge human nature. It is the truth sociobiology has to recommend and is crucial for person, planet and all creation. But as the early sociologists knew, accurate knowledge of human nature must transform our personal world views and society.

But notice how in Pinker's view, science and our worldviews do not have to change. Pinker does not want to have to change the place from which he sits. It is that objective perch. He wants intellectual life to be subservient to what he designates as the intentions of the genetic code. The sentence following his quote above says, "The alternative is to make intellectual life increasingly irrelevant to human affairs, to turn intellectuals into hypocrites, and to turn everyone into anti intellectuals." We must submit. But those are not the only two alternatives—anti-intellectualism or typical science. We could instead graduate to more mature thought and a different way of thinking about a human science that *begins* with values.

As Comte knew, acknowledging human nature *totally* overturns personal worldviews. The point isn't to remain a scientist and go, "oh golly," at the mystery of the universe. The point is to bring our knowledge to reflect back upon life and change the world. We must understand Comte's program for the Life Sciences. It is to use human knowledge to reduce suffering and improve human happiness.

And Pinker is transparently honest that he has nothing to replace the typical scientific paradigm. No wonder sociobiology is so resistant to Ortega y Gasset's crucial insight. Let me quote Ortega y Gasset at length because putting his original quote in context gives us great insight into what is wrong with sociobiology.

> Today we know that all the marvels of the natural sciences, inexhaustible though they be in principle, must always come to a full stop before the strange reality of human life. Why? If all things have given up a large part of their secret to physical science, why does this alone hold out so stoutly? The explanation must go deep, down to the roots. Perchance it is no less than this: that man is not a thing, that man has no nature (Ortega y Gasset , 1941: p. 185).

> Physico-mathematical reason . . . was in no state to confront human problems. By its very constitution it could do no other than search for man's nature. And naturally, it did not find it. human has no nature. Man is not his body, which is a thing, nor his soul, psyche, conscience, or spirit which are also things. Man is no thing, but a drama. (Ortega y Gasset, 1941, pp. 199-200).

> *man, in a word, has no nature; what he has is . . . history* (1941, p. 17)

> human life, it would appear then, is not a thing, has not a nature, and in consequence we must make up our minds to think of it in terms of categories and concepts that will be radically different from such as shed light on the phenomenon of matter (Ortega y Gasset, 1941, p. 186).

No wonder sociobiologists have to crucify Ortega y Gasset. It is unfortunate the word human "nature" allowed sociobiologists to be distracted from the crucial point that human beings are not things and must be studied with different methods than those used in the physical sciences. Human beings are more than just matter. The reason the human has held out so stoutly refusing to surrender its secrets is because the scientific view would obliterate the human. The hard sciences ignore questions of consciousness, belief, and values.

Ortega y Gasset's other point is quite succinct. We can't use human history to deduce human nature. There are certainly some basic human parameters of human existence which must always be addressed. But within the existential contingencies, there are a wide range of options. Perhaps, Ortega y Gasset was right—we shouldn't call it Human Nature because that would indicate it is a permanent state. And as Plato knew, human nature is not a matter of what is. It is becoming.

The Structure of Evil

We can't have a theory of human betterment without accounting for evil. But what do we do about evil? Conservatives say liberals don't understand evil. But actually liberals know far more about evil. Conservatives constantly avert their eyes. Conservatives want to quickly label people as evil and discard them—bomb them, throw them in prison. While they may dwell on gore to titillate like a tabloid or to coerce like a prosecutor seeking the death penalty, they don't want to take the time to understand the real human struggles that produced human evils. Evil gets projected over there as something foreign. Liberals have the same initial human knee jerk reactions as conservatives but have learned to pause to reflect and understand. Conservatives accuse them of being bleeding hearts. However, without sympathetic introspection, we can never understand human behavior.

Coming out of World War II there was a great deal of research by social scientists hoping to prevent it from ever happening again. We have discarded that research on authoritarianism, evil, the will to meaning, going along with the crowd and human destructiveness. Ruth Benedict who was part of that research once said she had "the faith of a scientist that behavior, no matter how unfamiliar to us, is understandable . . . and the faith of a humanist in the advantages of mutual understanding among men." (Mead, 1974: 75)

A Science of Humanity:

Drawing Conclusions from Knowledge

in Order to Make a Better World

There are core social and psychological processes at the center of existence. The desire for union. The need for differentiation. Conflict. Cooperation. Do we designate them as needs, drives or fundamental social processes? When Carl Jung was asked about the difference between gods and archetypes, being an honest man, he responded they were the same. We need such candid dialogue. Hal Pepinsky so brilliantly pinpoints the social dynamics of communication and conflict in *The Geometry of Democracy and Violence*. However, there was no need for him to ground them in the hard sciences (geometry) to improve credibility. It should have been enough to identify them as elementary social processes. Do you prefer to we say human needs are based on the existential contingencies of life or grounded in our biological makeup? We need honest dialogue to establish common ground. All that is necessary for a Science of Humanity is for us to agree on processes and components are fundamental. Psychology and Sociology has already covered this ground (although so many have forgotten).

How do we create a Science of Humanity? First, we must commence a conversation for that purpose. What can we conclude about the human condition?

To build a better world, I think we must begin with love, meaning (framework of orientation), and the need to be effective (Marx/Fromm's love of work, i.e. the need for productiveness). In other words, we need connectedness, the opportunity to be a star (a participant in our own lives) and social resources to help us live our dreams. Self esteem and synergy (win-win) should be our referents and evaluative standard. I think the case certainly can be made that lack of a subjective feeling of well being leads to all sorts of problems and that win-lose arrangements produce disastrous social consequences in the long run and are socially expensive to maintain Happiness is the only workable methodology. If we do not create a society promoting self esteem and synergy, we need to go back to the drawing board.

We would suggest these are more than our own personal opinions. We have learned something in 100 years of behavioral science about human behavior. As a social scientist, I conclude: Human beings want to feel good about themselves and to make sense of existence. We need love and human connection—to matter to someone and care about someone. Along with Maslow, Fromm and Becker, I concur there are some conclusions we should draw.

1. We are going to die. That is a biological truth. And from that stems the human need for meaning—to make sense of existence.

2. Alternatives exclude. Human beings need a framework to organize information and values in order to prioritize so we can act. Human needs provide an adequate foundation for human political agenda.

3. Cultural myths aside, we are connected and our lives depend upon others. We must find a way to share the world—both in cooperation and conflict—to get our needs met while acknowledging others' need to satisfy theirs. Self esteem and synergy should be our guidelines. The entire body of knowledge in sociology and psychology details the costs of ignoring this.

These provide the basis for a synthesis of the disciplines and the foundation for a Science of Humanity. With an agreement on any one of these three fundamentals of human existence, we can design a better world.

SECTION III

KNOWLEDGE FOR THE PEOPLE

Chapter 9:

The Foundations of

Humanistic Sociology[1]

Humanistic Sociology is not a difficult idea to define. For the humanistic sociologist, sociology is the study of how to make a better world. The key commitment is that people matter. As we noted in the introduction to this book, economist Kenneth Boulding (1977) said, "the question for the social sciences is
simply: what is better and how do we get there?" This is the conversation of humanistic sociology. It is a conversation about values. As a discipline we need to
be designing and implementing social systems for people rather than plugging
people into systems that don't understand or meet human needs. The question
becomes "What tools do we have, what knowledge do we possess, what understandings will ultimately make this world a better place for all people to live?"

   Humanistic sociology must be an exploration of effective social arrangements, institutions, and social forms which improve the conditions of living. Sociology is *for* people. We begin with analyzing human needs and then develop a
society that meets them. To use Comte's, Ward's, Small's, Lynd's, Sorokin's,
and Becker's idea: Sociology is a superordinate science in the service of humanity. To say it is a superordinate science means that it synthesizes the disciplines
and then uses that synthesis to forge a shared agreement about how to create a
better world. It is this idea that Comte meant to imply when he envisioned sociology as the "Queen of the Social Sciences."

   Ultimately, the quest must be to return mainstream sociology to its roots
which we would claim are humanism. However, many in the 1960s and 1970s
felt the need to break away from establishment sociology. Ironically, a year after
Al Lee was elected President of ASA by a write-in vote in 1975, he founded the
Association for Humanist Sociology. Rather than just representing another "fla-
vor" of academic sociology, humanism is a different paradigm. Humanistic sociology is about making a better world. What had become mainstream sociology
was the tame academic sociology. Humanistic sociology in the 1970s began in
the counterculture movement to envision alternative social forms, the reaction
against scientific sociology, the sociologies championed by Al Lee and John
Glass, and the foundations laid by humanistic psychologists including Abraham
Maslow and Erich Fromm. Other brands of sociology may contain eventual
"change the world" aspirations, but humanistic sociology brings that commitment right through the front door. While many traditional sociologists may con-
fess their values as biases, humanistic sociologists are die hard do-gooders and
proud of it.

Humanistic Sociology is not only an academic discipline, it is the merging of personal and professional identities. It is a methodology and theoretical perspective that is inner disciplinary in its delivery. We cannot afford to only be armchair observers. We have a critical stake in the human experiment.

The Two Sociologies

The best analysis of sociology ever written is Ernest Becker's *The Structure of Evil: An Essay on the Unification of the Science of Man.* We think the book should have probably been called "Making the Good," but that wouldn't have been seen as academically respectable. It provides a ready summary of the ground on which to trace the history of a humanistic sociology. Becker talks of the two sociologies. One is the superordinate science of humanity which calls us to action and to change the world. It is an ideal science concerned with not just "what is" but what "ought to be." The postmodernists have re-taught us that any version of "what is" contains its own recommendation of "what ought to be." August Comte and Lester Ward, in particular, knew this.

The second sociology is the narrow academic discipline content to color within the lines and seek only journal articles, research grants, and tenure. The first sociology is the original sociology of Comte, Marx, Ward, Small, and it is the change the world sociology to which Lynd, Sorokin, and C. Wright Mills invited us to return. Gouldner talked of the two Marxisms. It is the same distinction: one academic, one action oriented.

Armchair theorizing and coffee house speculation over society's puzzles and predicaments can paralyze us with inaction. A perpetual agenda of more research means action can be delayed forever. Lester Ward understood that piling up more and more facts will never get us to a science of humanity. Implementing a science of humanity is a matter of envisioning an ideal society and integrating the disciplines in the service of humanity. All knowledge is a power strategy. The question is: what kind of world do we want to construct? As Becker understood, sociology is an ideal type science—not in the narrow Weberian sense, but in the bold Comteian and Marxian sense of envisioning a better world. It is a utopian science.

The scientific stance was clearly expressed in Ogburn's 1929 ASA presidential address: "sociology is not interested in making the world a better place." This was a far cry from the ambitions of Albian Small when he founded the American Journal of Sociology. Albian Small said he launched *The American Journal of Sociology*:

> to translate sociology into the language of ordinary life, so it will not appear to be merely a classification and explanation of fossil fact . . . to so far increase our present intelligence about social utilities that there may be much more effective combination for the promotion of the general welfare . . . to insure the good of man." (AJS, 1895, pp. 13–14; both quoted in Becker, 1968: 73–74)

In 1886, John Eaton said: "Let the warning cry fill the air of scientific associations, from meeting to meeting, that science is our means, not our end." (quoted in Becker, 1968: 73) This is precisely the idea of Auguste Comte. The early sociologists did not see stacking up more and more knowledge as the sole task of sociology. They did not see it as accumulating data and laws that someone else might eventually apply for fair or foul. Becker uses Giddings as the archetype of the flaw of building sociology into a narrow academic discipline.

> It is easy to sum up Giddings fallacy: . . . by lifting an activist humanitarianism to the detached scientific heights of an opportunistic inductivism, we have lifted it right out of the world of contemporary social problems.

> The humanistic criticism of social values—radical in intent—bogs down practically into a conservatism of method that is self-defeating. . . . Sociology would thus be in the business as a disinterested discipline for a long time, and life would go on—and right by it. This is exactly what is happening today—Gidding's own legacy confirms the criticism of his orientation, and the penalty of the loss of an active, superordinate social science. (Becker, 1968: 77)

Humanism in Sociology—The Early Sociologists

Humanism in sociology is not new. Sociology has a history of do gooders. Many of early American sociologists were actually also ministers who came to sociology to perfect the art of implementing a Social Gospel. Social amelioration was the goal of most sociologists in the late 1880s.

In our rewriting of history, we often changed who many of the early sociologists were. Durkheim for example, is cast only as scientist. And yet this is the same Durkheim who noted that if someone comes up with an individualistic solution to a social problem, you can be sure that it is wrong. This is social agenda. It is implementing the sociological consciousness as a way of seeing social problems and solving them. Moving past individualistic explanations is as political as anything we will ever do. Comte and Ward in particular were well aware of this.

We have embraced positivism but rewritten what it means. As Becker notes, Comte coined the term "positivism" so he should be allowed to define it.

> By his own definition, Positivism meant *the subordination of politics to morals*. Science enters the picture *only to provide the basis for an agreed morality*.

> Thus, if science is centered on man and subserves him, and if progress is its goal, then, logically, when we find out the social causes of human unhappiness, we will have an automatic directive to an agreed solution. (Becker, 1968: 45)

However, as sociology moved to become a mere academic discipline, it shunned its roots based on real world problems. By the late 1920s and early 1930s it had

gained academic respectability. As mainstream sociology moved away from social betterment towards the academic version, every generation has produced its
critics. This loyal opposition has usually represented the voice of humanistic
sociology.

Robert Lynd and his wife Helen who authored the *Middletown* series were
among the preeminent pioneers of research on social class in America. However
in 1939, as the Germans marched across Europe enslaving all in their path, he
began to speak out against a sociology of human behavior isolated in the ivory
tower. We were collecting data, but what were we doing with all of those facts?
His *Knowledge for What?* proposed grounding sociology in attention to creating
a society that meets human needs. The story is told that as he presented his views
in lectures around the country, colleagues sat in the back rows and laughed at
him. They saw any effort to involve sociology in real world problems as a do
gooder return to unscientific superstition. They did not want to risk compromising the academic respectability and scientific status Sociology had fought so long
and hard to achieve.

Over in anthropology, Ruth Benedict was confronting the same dilemma
She talked of her ideas of synergy—the idea of a Good Society—freely in coffee
houses and even speeches but she was reluctant to publish her views because she
knew she would be accused of being unscientific. She had worked hard to promote the idea of cultural relativity. She knew she would be misunderstood, yet
everything she knew as a trained observer taught her that some social arrangements were factually better when viewed from *any human standpoint.* In some
cultures, people flourished. Other cultures were beset with overwhelming social
problems. Benedict's concern with cultural relativity is understandable. She had
stumbled upon the first concept which emerges when we move past value neutrality and relativity as the supreme goal.

Lynd and Benedict had excelled in their methods. But when they turned to
values and creating the good society, they were in danger of being trashed by
their colleagues. Pitirim Sorokin suffered similar treatment. His career towered
over half a century and he was the first chair of the Sociology department at
Harvard for a tenure lasting more than a decade. Sorokin was critical of the two
major trends he observed in modern sociology: towards either minutia (abstracted empiricism) or pomposity (grand theory). In the 1950s, he would found
the "Center for Creative Altruism" at Harvard and write several large volumes
on love and good neighbors. These works, of course, has long been forgotten in
sociology. If they are remembered, they are treated more as the indulgences of
an old man than the culmination of a life of study resulting in a creative bold
direction for sociology.

If we will remember, even August Comte met the same fate. We grudgingly
name him the father of the discipline but he has become a shadow figure in the
annals of sociology. We have rewritten history and as a result totally misunderstand his entire vision of sociology. For years teachers of social theory praised
Comte's work to build a scientific sociology but in the next breath have discounted his vision of sociology creating a better society. They often blame his
"love affair." It is interesting how the spin doctors trivialized things even back

then. Actually she was not some clandestine affair but a woman he loved deeply who died. Comte did not drift from his focus. His idea all along was to build a science of society and then implement it to make a better world. Her death simply made him more dedicated to his work and vision. He understood that sociology was in the business of envisioning the good society. As Becker tells the story:

> [Comte's] life's work is normally considered to fall into two distinct phases: the first work was a treatise on all sciences, putting forth the striking proposal that sociology followed logically in the history of the development of the sciences. . . . The second work enunciated the 'Religion of Humanity' based on love: in the new community, sociology would subserve the social order and be used to promote social interest instead of the private interest that was rampant. . . .
>
> Admirers of Comte based their admiration on the first work, and considered that the second work was done in the grip of dementia or senility. Often, they explicitly indict Comte's love affair with Clotilde de Vaux. We shall return to the reasoned and necessary unity of Comte's system; suffice it to say for now that, contrary to the opinion of many superficial commentators, Comte was well aware of what he was doing—the two 'phases' of his work were an integrated whole. The first period was a systematization that he undertook on a positivistic, scientific basis to avoid the charges of mysticism which he knew might be leveled against his guiding ideas. The second period was a frank predication of his life work on feeling, love, and morality, which he felt were the basis for his whole position. (Becker: 1968, 43–44)

Lester Ward also understood this. So did Albian Small who was chair of the first sociology department in the country—the University of Chicago. The early sociologists envisioned an applied academy that would improve people's lives.

Today in our sociological theory classes, we have claimed George Herbert Mead as a sociologist but we don't include other Chicago School members such as Mead's colleague in philosophy John Dewey or his partner in social action Jane Addams. Furthermore, we have only allowed Mead into the club because we have sanitized Mead. When we think of Mead, we think of an arm chair theorist. We don't think of the person who led Women's Rights marches in Chicago or was an active participant in Hull House. But even if we only read Mead's social theories, we don't understand them unless we recognize that they are bent on social action for social betterment. In Mead's theory: we are part of the same over all drama and entwined in each other's fate. He felt that development of a "Generalized Other" would lead to a sane society based on empathy and love. He saw the sociological consciousness as intimately tied to social action. It is similar to the theme of the interrelation between individual troubles and social problems that had been Comte's original concern.

John Dewey, who offered an outfront pragmatism that in some ways is similar to the real Mead, was too obviously action oriented for later scientific scholars to claim him as a sociologist. And of course, Jane Addams herself was kicked out of the field so to speak. She was relegated to a "women's role" of social helper and a discipline called Social Work created to keep her type away from the rational, masculine science of "real" sociology. Sociology was being defined as a narrow academic discipline. However, Dewey and Addams wouldn't have seen it this way. Neither would have George Herbert Mead or W.I. Thomas who were their colleagues at Hull House and the University of Chicago. Even though Ernest Burgess had a hand in the academic and scientific legitimization of sociology, he was also clearly concerned with social action and social betterment. He was not only an admirer of Jane Addams but led the city's social action committee on homelessness. All this should say that Humanistic Sociology has a rich and ongoing tradition in sociology. It would be right at home in the Chicago School of sociology.

Humanistic Psychology

Erich Fromm and Abraham Maslow were founding voices of humanistic psychology. Psychology before them had focused only upon individuals with problems rather than the healthy personality.

Prior to Fromm and Maslow, we knew almost nothing about the healthy personality. The only people who showed up in therapists' office and got studied were sick people. Thus, the literature of the field abounded with stories about the abnormal and seldom gave a second glance at those who were not experiencing severe problems in everyday life. Indeed, Freud had hypothesized a healthy personality but it was a negative definition—someone who had made it through the oral, anal, and oedipus phases stages without getting stuck. Fromm would say that medical students spend more time studying cadavers than living healthy human beings and noted psychological knowledge also focused only on sickness rather mental health.

Maslow would talk about self actualization. Rogers would talk about "self realization." Fromm called the same thing the unfolding of human power, productivity, or aliveness. In fact Nietzsche is sometimes referred to as the Father of Humanistic Psychology because of his focus on what he called the actualizing tendency. The "be all that you can be" slogan that the Army ripped off in their ad promotions actually does a nice job of summarizing the viewpoint of humanistic psychology. Victor Frankel's *Will to Meaning* and Fromm in *Man For Himself* emphasized that making sense of existence is paramount to human beings.

Freud in *Civilization and Its Discontents* had seen an inevitable opposition between the individual and society. Humanistic psychology saw something different. Psychology began to realize that the social context in which interaction takes place matters. For instance, Karen Horney wrote *The Neurotic Personality* in which she contended that society itself had become sick. Erich Fromm in *The Sane Society* took a similar approach.

Traditionalists would talk about creating people for society. Humanists, on the other hand, would focus on creating society for people, arguing that social arrangements and social institutions should function for the human. In the 1950s, psychology departments taught courses on the "Psychology of Adjustment." By the early 1970s, these courses had become the "Healthy Personality." This is an important distinction. In 1958, publishers insisted on entitling Sidney Jourard's book on the healthy personality: *Personal Adjustment: An Approach Through The Study Of Healthy Personality.* By 1974, he was finally allowed to title what amounted to a revised third edition *Healthy Personality: An Approach from the Viewpoint of Humanistic Psychology.*

Jourard has particular insights for overcoming alienation in bureaucracies and humanizing organizations. His work on *The Transparent Self* and self disclosure is the perfect antidote to the role player who has lost his or her soul to the game. To create humanistic organizations, we must behave as full people rather than surrender identities merely to a cultural or organization role. Jourard says that the lack of dialog is the crisis of our time. We need to develop role distance and begin to wear our roles lightly. To worship cultural myths is idolatry. It also means that we sacrifice our authentic self to the role we think we are supposed to play.

Humanistic psychology had the need for a companion humanistic sociology that could focus on the conditions of life enhancement. Under some conditions people flourish while under others although the spirit is willing, people atrophy. A Humanistic Sociology would ask questions such as: "What type of environment produces psychological healthy, happy people? What types of social resources are helpful to people in their struggles and make it more likely they will thrive?" Sociology today still focuses upon social problems rather than the healthy society or social solutions. Concluding his book *Building Community: Social Science in Action,* Phillip Nyden of Loyola University's community research notes that while every sociology department has courses in Social Problems, none have courses on Social Solutions. There is a twin frontier on the human potential. It is self and it is community. We must concur with Immauel Kant who envisioned the ideal as "maximum individuality within maximum community."

The Beginnings of a Formal Humanistic Sociology

To the layperson, the term "humanistic sociology" would seem redundant. It would seem obvious that sociology is concerned with the person and human needs. But sociology has drifted from its original intent and purpose and it was now necessary to specify a specially *humanistic* sociology.

C. Wright Mills certainly sought to define a discipline quite different from the confines of scientific sociology. He saw an engaged discipline confronting the powers that be to provide space for the human. Joseph Scimecca (1995) sees the origins of humanist sociology in Mills' conceptions emphasized human power and confronting the power elite which limits freedom and meaning. Scimecca also firmly credits Ernest Becker's emphasis on self esteem as an important building block for a humanist sociology.

Historically, humanistic sociology originates in the reaction and critique against a value-free scientific sociology, and in the counterculture movement to create alternative social forms. A few sociologists have spoken formally of the possibility of a "humanistic sociology" that would depart from existing theoretical approaches. In *Humanistic Society*, John Glass and John Staude (1972) compiled the theoretical ground which might provide the starting point for a humanistic sociology. John Glass would go on to found the Clinical Sociology Association which later became the Sociological Practice Association. Alfred McClung Lee (1973) in *Toward Humanist Sociology* argued that the best sociology has always been humanistic and that the paradigm included the works of classic scholars: Cooley, Thomas, Sorokin, and Mills.

Lee (1973: 180–201) suggests sociologists can perform an important service to humanity by breaking down the traditional barriers that have plagued effective action by academicians to make a better world.

> The excuse for the existence of sociologists is not simply the maintenance of academic employment and research funding. The chief excuse is the answering of the question, 'Sociology for whom?' in this manner: Sociology for the service of humanity. This answer refers to the need to develop knowledge and direct service to all classes of people as citizens, as consumers, and as neighbors. This means knowledge of social behavior that can and will be communicated by its developers through all appropriate media to those who can best use it. It includes studies of ways in which people can protect themselves from undesirable manipulation by those in positions of power, of how to achieve more livable homes and communities, of constructive alternatives to family, civil, and international violence, and of much more. [1978: 36]

As long as one deals with theories and governmentally-funded studies, one does not have to risk soiling personal clothing. Sociologists might go about inventing or changing the real world through personal involvement. Lee championed using a variety of public outlets including writings, lecturing, media presentations for sociologists to get the message across. Lee viewed the individual as the element through which society is changed and envisioned (Lee, 1978: 28–53). Sociology thus needs to debunk myths and change people's minds:

> In serving humanity, sociologists act principally as critics, demystifiers, reports, and clarifiers. They review critically the folk wisdom and other theories by which people try to live. In doing so, they strip away some of the outwork clutter of fictions about life and living that make the human lot even more difficult than it might be. Then they try to report more accurate information about the changing social scene and with it to help clarify ways of understanding human relations and of coping with personal and social problems. (1973: 36)

Reaction Against Value-Free Science

Several decades ago C.P. Snow warned that we were becoming two cultures, one scientific and one humanistic. The scientific approach treats people as objects, as means. The humanistic approach values people as ends in themselves. Our means and ends must correlate. Science would simply tack values on at the end of what otherwise was a scientific process. Humanism would begin with values and human purposes. Scientific knowledge views the human as separate and just an object for study. Humanism sees the human as intimately entwined in the whole process of conscious and knowing.

The move to science has been a curious adventure. Science was not seen as a human act but was simply viewed as a neutral, objective process. We pretend that the scientific act of looking isn't a part of human behavior: the world just *appears* before our lenses. Please note the shift: we refuse to pay any attention to our act of viewing (what going on "In Here") and pretend we are just objectively seeing the "Out There." As we move from physical science to social science, we then turn our objective scientific lenses back upon ourselves to view human behavior. You can't refuse to acknowledge that science is a human act and then utilize our constructed mechanical science to understand the human. We can't decide to view the "Out There" by denying the "In Here" and then turn around and use such a method to view the "In Here." It doesn't make any sense. But that is what a human science that uses only the scientific method does. Followers utilize a method that denies the existence of human consciousness and then use that method to view human consciousness. Psychologist Carl Jung in the early 1900s would claim that the central problem of the age was to recover the intuitive, feminine, right brain aspects of self and culture. He felt that if science were to continue to advance without such synthesis, it would leave behind the human.

With the scientific consciousness, the world itself had changed. Not only did we think and deal with the world in scientific terms, but the world was deemed identical with these scientific terms. The earth became a *thing*. It is this "I–It" brand of knowledge that has such grave consequences. The metaphors of Nature were replaced with mechanical scientific metaphors. The world was tamed, it was explainable, and carved to this image. This is reification in its purest sense: We created an idea of the world and then shaped the world to this artificial image. A walk in the woods no longer meant what it once had: children marched out from the classroom not to smell a flower but to count its petals; the trees became timber for harvest; the rocks became mineral resources, and the forest itself and the land changed. It was logged and paved with roads. Cities with factories were erected on the most scenic spots. The world was made manageable and fitted to the scientific vision. As one sociologist commented on the Army Corp of Engineers, their vision must be "if it moves, pave it."

When science turned its view to a social science and a psychological science, it continued to territorialize the unknown. As Freud proclaimed: "Where Id was, let Ego be." The problem is that as more and more of the human became rationalized in our theories and institutionalized in scientific bureaucratic organizations, there became less and less room for the movement of the human. As science territorialized more of the world with its left brain techniques, the human was left to retreat into smaller and smaller realms. As Jung knew so well, a complete scientific "success" would mean the elimination of the human. Rationality and left brain technologies would stamp out right brain feelings and values. *The crucial humanistic conversation is to find ways of thinking and ways of managing that allow room for the human spirit.*

Science has minimized or trivialized all that does not fit its worldview. Anything that resembles magic or mystery has long ago been chased from the world and relegated inside the psyche: feelings got stuffed inside, magic became mere mood, visions became projection. Awe and wonder were but fleeting emotions of the untrained. Religion became a soothing opiate and love was deemed an expedient by-product. God was relegated to a far corner in the universe and it made no difference whether we used the word "God" or "Nature" in our theories. Even the human heart became only a "black hole" in an otherwise scientific reality.

The early scientists sought to stamp out the irrational. Everything that did not fit the scientific reality was swept from easy view: feelings, intuitions, love. Francis Bacon who was also Grand Inquisitor of England during the witch hunts claimed Knowledge should be tamed into Power. He modeled science after a witch hunt actually suggesting Nature should be stretched on the rack and tortured until she reveals her secrets (Merchant, 1980). Obviously the feminine was not placed in high regard.

Having tamed the wilderness, paved the landscape, and harnessed natural resources, science then looked for new worlds to conquer. As Science turned its gaze to human behavior, human beings were soon left alienated from the world.

Science sought a "knowledge" of nature separate from the human "observer." It achieved such a vision and legislated such a world. Humans were left as passive consumer; creatures caught in the maze of a mechanical universe. The self-fulfilling prophecy of science had been realized at a terrible cost. This separation of the human from nature was worse than even the earlier mind-body split.

The world had changed and we did not feel at home in it. Our way of viewing each other became colored by the scientific lens. Science depends upon doubt, testing, and making things prove themselves. We might wonder if there are not some realities which depend upon our willing suspension of disbelief. A value-free science is incapable of providing us with a world containing meaning. It is no wonder humans were left alienated from the world and from life itself, we were cast as strangers to the whole process. Science has constructed a world separate from human values and purposes. With such an objectivity, the human element could only appear as an anomaly: a "freak" exception in an otherwise scientific process. Lacking any "real world" canopy which would cover the human, we were soon alienated from the world, each other, and ourselves. Humanistic sociology would return the human to center stage.

Determinism—The Soul of Science

Charles Hampden Turner (1970) in *Radical Man* says that the toolbox we have borrowed from science posits a Conservative vision of humanity. The dream of science is to render everything explainable: to eliminate and explain all variation. It is a dream of complete control. Science seeks to make everything predictable: to make us "safe" from the human. It gives credibility to and values the static, the fixed, the predictable. At its core, it aims to eliminate the human from the process. Ultimately, its goal would change the nature of what we call "human." Dennis Wrong argued our idea of the oversocialized person who is totally predictable is not the vision of a free society; nor is it good social science.

It is small wonder that the romantic poets sprang to life at the very time, Science was beginning its heyday. They originated in direct reaction against Science. Intuitively, they saw something in science that was taking humanism out of humanity. To a person, the romantic poets wailed against science. Mary Shelley would write the novel *Frankenstein* about the abuses of a science in which curiosity had lost its soul. William Blake went so far as to claim that Science was the Anti-Christ.

We might wonder what would cause them to invoke such an extreme characterization? The romantic poets saw science as torturing the awe, mystery, and wonder out of life. Science was rendering the world dead—or at least under control–in order to do its analytical dissection. With the scientific world view, all was to be explainable. Mystery would vanish. Nature was tamed. Power was harnessed. However, despite the practicality of technological inventions, something got lost.

As the poet Wordsworth said,

> Sweet is the lore that Nature brings;
> Our meddling instinct
> Mis-shapes the beauteous forms of things
> we murder to dissect

Fromm maintained there are two ways of knowing. One path is the autopsy table of science:

> In children we often see this path to knowledge quite overtly. The child takes something apart, breaks it up in order to know it; or it takes an animal apart; cruelly tears off the wings of a butterfly in order to know it, to force its secret. The cruelty itself is motivated by something deeper: the wish to know the secret of things and of life . . . . The other path to knowing 'the secret is love. (Fromm, 1956, p. 25)

Maslow in *The Psychology of Science* says Buber's "I–Thou" represents a humanistic way of knowing rather than typical objective science. The other way of knowledge, "I–It," turns everything into an object for manipulation: rocks, trees, and ultimately, people.

Objectivity would have us pretend that humans are not doing the observing: it thus avoids problems of human consciousness. It demands an alienation between the "'In-Here" and the "Out-There": between the human and the object of study.

Theodore Roszak in *Makings of a Counterculture: Technological Society and Its Youthful Opposition* (1969) wrote,

> whatever its epistemological status . . . objectivity as a state of being fills the
> very air we breathe in a scientific culture . . . the mentality of the ideal scientist
> becomes the very soul of the society (Roszak, 1969, p. 216).

> Objective consciousness is alienated life promoted to its most honorific status
> as scientific method. Under its auspices, we subordinate nature to our com-
> mand only by estranging ourselves from more and more of what we experience
> . . . (Roszak, 1969, p. 232).

> when we challenge the finality of objective consciousness as basis for culture,
> what is at issue is the size of man's life. We must insist that a culture which ne-
> gates or subordinates or degrades visionary experience commits the sin of di-
> minishing our existence. Which is precisely what happens when we insist that
> reality is limited to what objective consciousness can turn into the stuff of sci-
> ence . . . (Roszak, 1969, p. 234).

Maslow says that awe and wonder were actually originally the crucial part of the
scientific experience. However, our rational pretense meant the submission of
awe and wonder, of imagination and reverence for life to a secondary status.
Mystery has disappeared. Roszak continues:

> One cliched argument suggests that the work of the scientist begins with the
> poet's sense of wonder (a dubious hypothesis at best) but then goes beyond it
> armed with spectroscope and light meter. The argument misses the key point:
> the poet's experience is defined precisely by the fact that the poet does not go
> beyond it. . . . Or are we to believe it was by failure of intelligence that Words-
> worth never graduated into the status of weatherman? (Roszak, 1969, p. 253)

Humanism in many ways is a reverse image of the scientific model. Love is not
objective and detached, it is involved and concerned. Rather than doubt and testing, it speaks of truths that only reveal themselves with trust and commitment.
Instead of prediction, manipulation and control, humanism respects the person.
Humanistic power is about influence, creating resources, and empowering people. Rather than value-free, humanism is a commitment to human welfare and
social betterment.

Buber offers us the way out of our dilemma. He speaks of a twin process of
consciousness: (1) the setting at distance which is necessary for perception, and
(2) the reuniting of the separated. This is similar to Paul Tillich work in *Love,
Power, and Justice* as well as the philosophy of Erich Fromm in *The Art of Loving* and his other works. As long as the two fold process occurs, we are in touch
with our humanity. However, when the setting at a distance is reified as an ideal
objectivity, then we have solid separated ourselves from each other and turned
the other into a permanent "It" or object. So much of this also is akin to George
Herbert Mead's conception of the "I" and the "me" as an ongoing process.

As Maslow notes, we must take advantage of both ways of knowing if our
knowledge is to be complete. This doesn't mean we do traditional science and

then do humanism in our off duty hours. It means we need to reconceptualize science and formulate a humanistic science that embraces both ways of knowing.

Once we enthrone objectivity, we have separated ourselves from each other. Once we institutionalize ourselves too tightly into the role player ("the me"), we lose the transparency of an authentic self and the fluidity of movement back and forth between the "I" and the "me."

Ironically, while the actual physical sciences moved to a paradigm of relativity following Einstein and Heisenberg, sociology embraced old line deterministic science. Ideas such as cause and effect, explaining away all variation, and prediction and control dominate modern social science. Modern physics may have developed theories which look more like an old episode of *Star Trek* where each system defines its own time and space, but sociological science is still back with a Newtonian paradigm.

Einstein's favorite philosopher, Emile Meyerson characterized August Comte as that "inspired madman." His vision of a science where politics was subjugated to morals was truly inspired. Science would provide the basis for agreement on the conditions under which human beings flourish. However, Meyerson argued a predictive science that seeks total control and total explanation is ultimately absurd. It would seek to reduce everything to identity: this variable is really explainable by this, and that is explainable by that etc. . . . Science according to Meyerson is really slow motion common sense and ultimately thinking will not free us from the responsibility of having to decide and implement values.

A post Newtonian social science could certainly be conceived where each set of value decisions define their own universe and consequences. We see this as precisely what pragmaticism sought to do. It is also the hope of a mature postmodern science. However, we do not see this conception of science emerging yet as a major sociological alternative yet. A humanistic science to which Maslow aspired is very different from the deterministic mode in which modern social science has cast its lot.

Changing the scientific roadmap is critical. It is our way of organizing our thoughts and it is also our way of organizing people in organizations. If humanism is to survive we must reorganize both our thinking and our organizations to make room for the human.

Counterculture Movement

Science replaced the sacred foundation of culture based on myth, magic, and mystery with a secular foundation emphasizing history, technology, and reason.

> The transformation is blunt and bold: one Reality Principle knocking its predecessor for a loop . . . the great reversal has been the total *secularization* of culture in mind and deed—certainly the most potent, daring, and original project of modern times, as well as the most distinctive historical contribution of Western society (Roszak, 1975, pp. 159–160).

There has been no appreciation by advocates of science for the fact that by such a process something crucial is lost. What is lost is the humanistic ethos! We treat love and the magical only as anomalies—exceptions in an otherwise scientific world view. The magical becomes mere mood or feeling. Love finds no room in the halls of scientific bureaucracy.

Theodore Roszak (1969) originally coined the term "counterculture" in a book entitled *The Makings of a Counterculture: Technological Society and Its Youthful Opposition*. Roszak saw rational science as an inadequate basis for culture. Youthful alienation was a natural byproduct of a technological culture with little room for the human. The counterculture itself set about attempting to create new social forms and social institutions that would overcome alienation. People were called to function as an artist inventing their own lives and society.

Not only did the counterculture involve sociological ideas, but it involved many people who were sociologists. Indeed students then came to sociology to change the world. We must not forget that the campus student protests of the 1960s and early 1970s were a movement largely brought about and "sponsored" by sociology. It was sociology teachers who were talking about the Vietnam War and the need to restructure society and to rethink our values. Fully fifty percent of Berkeley campus demonstrators were sociology majors (Lipset and Wolin). This was a fact not lost on the Nixon administration which then worked to cut funding to sociology departments.

When former Columbia student activist James Kunen, who wrote *The Strawberry Statement,* was asked what happened to the counterculture movement, he said, "They stole our symbols." The Madison Avenue capitalistic machine could mass market blue jeans, peace signs, and protest music as well as anything else. Get yourself a t-shirt and be a hippie too. When everybody's a hippie, nobody's a hippie. It didn't matter to the corporate establishment what decal you put on your t-shirt, or what message was in the lyrics of the music as long as you bought it with good hard cash. Capitalism is amazingly flexible. As media visionary Marshall McLuhan warned us: "The medium is the message." The content is almost irrelevant. The counterculture became a fad and went the way of all fads: it passed out of fashion.

When Roszak (1979, 1980) was asked what became of the counterculture movement, he claimed it won. It became enfranchised in a historically new normative ethic of personhood. Self fulfillment became a right. We had always talked about the pursuit of happiness, but generations before embraced the cultural value of "self denial" and "self sacrifice." The counterculture made self-exploration a legitimate rhetoric of motive.

Roszak was both right and wrong. The counterculture was routinized into American society by emphasizing the psychological and neglecting the sociological. The psychological focus on personal fulfillment became a part of the American cultural mythos, but the movement to create new alternative social forms and social institutions was rejected and ultimately negated. By institutionalizing only the psychological aspects, the routinized counterculture led to abuses of self-indulgence and the over-concern with self. The insight of personal power that you create your own reality became a mandate rather than a doorway.

Ironically, it actually became part of the conservative backlash which then and today focuses on the myth of individualism, individual responsibility and denies the plight of the other. The only difference between the alienation that characterizes youth yesterday with the alienation today is that once we actually thought we'd change things. However, without an effective social canopy which empowers youth in a meaningful drama, we are left growing up as absurd as ever. We must realize that it is not just the individual creating their own reality but that we do it within the context of available social resources. The sociological understanding is not that just "I" create reality but that "we" create reality together.

The other good answer to the question of "what became of the counterculture?" is that it became the Women's Movement. Bill always thought that the counterculture died one night on the late night *Tonight Show with Johnny Carson*. Students for Non-Violence Coalition Committee Co-Chair Stokely Carmichael who had coined the words "Black Power" was asked: "What positions are available to women in the movement?" Carmichael who is normally a very intellectual, persuasive, urbane gentleman said, "The only position for women is prone." It was an obscene sexist joke, but the audience at the time laughed.

Women had marched on Selma. They had been killed at Kent State. They had sat down on buses. They had worked with their brothers throughout the movement. But despite this movement to human freedom, women were clearly regarded as second class citizens. What happened to the counterculture? We always thought women went right on changing. Men were only willing to go so far. Shere Hite talks about *Women and Love: A Cultural Revolution in Progress.* A cultural revolution is when we change the story. Women were changing. Men soon sat the revolution out. They hadn't bargained for it changing their power relationships with women.

It is also no coincidence that the women's movement occurred historically at the same time that the self personal psychology movement evolved. The two are actually part of the same movement. Women had always been taught to sacrifice self for others. Self love was a new virtue. "I am a person. I am also important." As Gloria Steinem wrote: *Revolution from Within: The Politics of Self Esteem.* The women's movement redefined love and self.

Unfortunately, the larger capitalistic culture was right on guard to try and insure that changes would only effect individuals rather than transform all social institutions. We have divided the world into masculine and feminine qualities and then we have systematically devalued the feminine. Traditionally, the masculine has been rational, thinking, scientific. The feminine has been caring, feeling, humanistic. We need to revision both our ways of organizing information (our theories) and our ways of organizing people (our organizations and ways of governing). The Scientific compromise with humanistic values has always been quite simple: leave humanism at home confined to a day of rest and allow rational science to determine how we shape the world. It is the old dialectic of the mind-body split, think-feeling and masculine—feminine. It is also the dichotomy of what we have traditionally felt belongs at work and what belongs at home. We left love and humanistic values out of the practical marketplace and political conversations. The "real world" we have made in the left brain, masculine, rational, scientific image. Feminism ultimately means not just female bodies in the work place but re-structuring the way we do business and government alike.

> When women enter the system as it stands, those who succeed will do so by adapting to it—by being competitive, by submerging their interpersonal, humanistic and supportive qualities. . . . Is achievement of *his* lifestyle to be the goal of a great social revolution of human liberation? . . . Freed from sexist values, we, as a society, could conceivably strive under the leadership of women to alter the priorities and styles of our institutions in order to foster the psychological development of each individual, the relationships of people with other people, and the relationship of people with their institutions. What we must accomplish is the reverse of the direction in which we are sliding. The worthwhile and extraordinary revolution would be one in which the objectives and styles historically associated with *women* become those of society are associated with *people*. (Bardwick, 1979: 174)

We need a new synthesis between the masculine and the feminine. We have discarded and devalued the feminine. It is only natural that we must now celebrate and revalue the feminine which has been lost. Having divided the world into two categories, masculine and feminine, ultimately we must reintegrate them in a new synthesis which preserves the best of both. This means a new marriage between thinking and feeling; between rational science and values.

Humanism would set about remaking the world so we cared about self and about each other. The counterculture originally spawned such a vision. The larger culture routinized it and we detoured.

Perhaps, sociology should be an art instead of a science. Nesbit had held that sociology is an art. But he didn't really mean it. His classic article "Sociology as Art" is really about the role of the intuitive in hypothesis formularization. Otherwise, he is clinging to a scientific process.

The counterculture offered a preview of the directions sociology might take. It seems to have pinpointed the questions for a humanistic sociology as art: How do we create social forms which empower people? How do we create society for people instead of people for society? *Our social constructions should function for the human—not mold the human to some other purpose.* This is the meaning of humanism in sociology. Sociology must be an art creating new social forms.

Humanistic sociology seeks to overcome alienation and establish social institutions where the human spirit and wonder can flourish. It also strives to confront the forces of de-humanization and depersonalization which would enslave us.

Humanistic Epistemology

Martin Buber contrasts between "I–Thou" relationships and "I–It" relationships. An "I–Thou" relationship realizes that the other person has a full humanity just like yourself. Humanists are not willing to just turn others into objects. We cannot settle for theories that reduce people to less than what they are. As humanists, we can settle for nothing less than full humanity.

We must respect the humanity of the other person. They are also a "thou," just like us. They are also struggling with the predicaments of life. Mark Carey (2001) the former director of probation for the state of Minnesota said he wanted a sense of humility in probation officers: a feeling that there but for fortune go I.

Lovers must also respect the humanity in the other person. If I just force a lover, then it is not love. It is closer to rape or prostitution. Parents have a similar dilemma. They want their child to be free and to have their own identity. They also want the child to do what they want. If a child always does what their parents want, then freedom is only hypothetical and is untested.

For the humanist, our means must reflect our ends. Our means cannot violate our image of the human. As humanists, we must respect our subjects. As humanistic sociologists, we must opt for social forms that empower humanity rather than techniques for some to manipulate and control others.

If we study the forest, the redwood trees, and wildlife, do we not have some sensitivity and caring that what we are studying should survive? Humanists begin with a commitment to humanity. We cannot opt for a science which diminishes or reduces our humanity.

It may sound strange, but perhaps we must discuss the theology of our brand of sociology. Theologians would claim that a loving God allows free will and therefore does not control the outcome. A loving God values the human. A loving social science must do the same. A humanistic social science cannot opt for prediction and control that destroys free will and the human.

Humanistic sociology departs from the narrow scientific epistemology which seeks prediction and control. In *The Psychology of Science*, Maslow writes:

> The ultimate goals of knowledge about persons are different from the goals of knowledge about things and animals. . . . If humanistic science may be said to have any goals beyond sheer fascination with the human mystery and enjoyment of it, these would be to release the person from external controls and to make him *less* predictable to the observer (to make him freer, more creative, more inner-determined) even though perhaps more predictable to himself. (Maslow, 1966: p. 40)

Indeterminacy

If we allow people freedom, who knows what will happen? We can't control the outcome. As Ernest Becker (1968, p. 364) notes, "opting for man as an end . . . means introducing indeterminacy into the world. One must have a firm faith in man, in his potential for increasingly ethical action." Humanism refuses to conceive of human beings as smaller role-like versions ripe for manipulation. However, if we are to empower people, we must ultimately trust the person. If people are ends and not merely means, then we have no absolute power over them. We cannot control the outcome. At its very core, humanism introduces indeterminacy into the equation.

Humanistic power provides a very different road than the scientific power of force, control and determinism. We value the person rather than treating people as objects for manipulation. The research on children who beat the odds and rise out of at risk environments shows they tend to have mothers who believed there was something special in the child. Rather than just mold to a purpose, they listened to the child.

Maslow's critique of science was at least as important as his idea of self actualization. Sociology must examine its moral epistemology. A sociology where knowledge is based on being able to predict and control people is morally suspect. Value neutral techniques which can then be used for fair or foul, will not suffice. Whom do we serve? This is the dilemma that Alvin Gouldner warned about in *The Coming Crisis in Western Sociology*. It is also the warning of Alfred McClung Lee's *Sociology for Whom?* As Becker questions, do we want a sociology that masters the art of enslaving? If we build a deterministic science that allows prediction and control, it will be used.

Humanistic Power

Carl Rogers (1977) said he had always thought of power as power over things or the ability to force one's will on another. When someone said his psychology was about power, it took him a long time to understand that they were right. He was talking about personal power.

The humanistic power is not force and compulsion. It is the power of actualized being. Nietzsche spoke of it as "the will to power." This is why Nietzsche is sometimes referred to as the "Father of Humanistic Psychology." He gives us a different ontology of power—the humanistic power. Power in this sense is the will to life.

> basically the will to power in Nietzsche is . . . a designation of the dynamic self-affirmation of life. It is, like all concepts describing ultimate reality, both literal and metaphorical. The same is true of the meaning of power in the concept the 'will to power.' It is not the sociological function of power which is meant . . . enforcing one's will against social resistance, is not the content of the will to power. The latter is the drive of everything living to realize itself with increasing intensity and extensity. The will to power is not the will of men to attain power over men, but it is the self-affirmation of life in its self-transcending dynamics, overcoming internal and external resistance. This interpretation of Nietzsche's 'will to power' easily leads to a systematic ontology of power (Tillich, 1954, p. 36).

Humanistic conceptions of power differ radically from the scientific power of cause and effect. We cannot successfully treat the human with the same mechanical tools we have used in the physical sciences: "That which is forced must preserve its identity. Otherwise, it is not forced but destroyed. . . . One cannot transform a living being into a complete mechanism, without removing its centre and this means without destroying it as a living unity" (Tillich, 1954, p. 46).

Nietzsche spoke of freedom *for* things as opposed to freedom *from* things. He noted that when most people use the word freedom, they are speaking as if they meant *freedom from,* but what they really desire is *freedom for:* the ability, the opportunity to accomplish some purpose. Power can also be conceived of in this way. Power *for* is the humanistic power and relates to actualization. Power *from* or power *over* is the scientific power which needs control and domination. Fromm (1947) used this same distinction to develop his conceptions. He termed them power *of* and power *over:*

> Power of = capacity, and power over = domination. This contradiction, however is of a particular kind. Power = domination results from a paralysis of power = capacity. 'Power over' is the perversion of 'power to'. . . . Domination is coupled with death, potency with life (p. 94).

Fromm (1947, p. 98) noted that this conception was also not foreign to the thinking of Spinoza (Ethics IV, Def. 8) who wrote that "by virtue and power, I understand the same thing." *The humanistic power is the power of actualized being.* Charisma is the personal power. *It is an attraction to realized living.* We are attracted towards the humanistic power. We do not need to be forced, but willingly join the dance.

In the discussion of the ontology of power, we are going to have to include theologian Paul Tillich. He and Fromm clearly read and were influenced by each other. It is sometimes hard to distinguish who came up with which idea. Tillich also was firmly in personal dialog with Maslow. Tillich expands these same concepts in *Love, Power, and Justice.* For Tillich, like Fromm, love means overcoming separateness: two people becoming one. Fromm would call it "fusion under conditions of integrity." Power is the actualizing power, it is the life force, it is realized being. This is the same as Maslow's, Fromm's, and Nietzsche's understanding. Justice is being just to oneself. It is recognizing the other person. It is what Fromm would call "respect", which from the original Latin means "to look at," to see someone—not as who you want them to be—but who they really are. It is perhaps the grain of truth in the scientific idea of objectivity. It is the commitment to be honest, not to falsify. Respect allows someone to be who they are.

Love is overcoming separateness: two people becoming one. Justice or respect, is two people being two—each having their own identities. As Martin Buber said, these two twin processes are inseparable. We must have one to have the other. It is setting at a distance and then overcoming the separateness.

Tillich (1954) proceeded to argue that conceiving of love as overcoming separateness implied that co-dependent relationships which dilute individuals into partial persons cannot, by definition be love.

> Love is the drive for reunion of the separated. It presupposes that there is something to be reunited, something relatively independent that stands upon itself. Sometimes the love of complete self-surrender has been praised and called the fulfillment of love. But the question is: What kind of self-surrender is it and what is it that it surrenders? If a self whose power of being is weakened or vanishing surrenders, his surrender is worth nothing. . . . The surrender of such an emaciated self is not genuine love because it extinguishes and does not unite what is estranged. The love of this kind is the desire to annihilate one's responsible and creative self for the sake of the participation in another self which by the assumed act of love is made responsible for himself and oneself. The chaotic self-surrender does not give justice to one's own power of being and to ac-

cept the claim for justice which is implied in this power. *Without this justice there is no reunitive love, because there is nothing to unite* (Tillich, 1954, pp. 68–69).

Buber's "I—Thou" offers a different paradigm to Science. It provides a framework where overcoming separateness and love can take place. As long as the world and others are frozen as objects, such reunion cannot be achieved.

Love is infinitely social. It is between an I and a Thou. It requires respect for the identity of each. It requires the uniting across the distance. And it requires a social relationship and a way of organizing self with room for actualization. How do we create social arrangements with room for the hand of life to move?

If we are going to talk about humanistic sociology, then we have to talk about love. It is the core value in a humanistic conception. Love invites. We cannot force love. We cannot move past a person's defenses into love unless the person allows us. The other person must be willing to entertain love. Abraham Maslow's (1962) discussion of growth shows this aspect of the humanistic power quite clearly:

> Defensiveness can be as wise as daring; it depends on the particular person, his particular status and the particular situation in which he has to choose. The choice of safety is wise when it avoids pain that may be more than the person can bear at the moment. If we wish to help him grow, then all we can do is help if he asks for help out of suffering, or else simultaneously allow him to feel safe and beckon him onward to try the new experience like the mother whose arms invite the baby to try to walk. We can't force him to grow, we can only coax him to, make it possible for him, in the trust that simply experiencing the new experience will make him prefer it; no one can prefer it for him. If it is to become part of him, he must like it. If he doesn't, we must gracefully concede that it is not for him at this moment (p. 54).

This reminds one of the battered woman trying to get out of her circumstances. We must continually offer an outstretched hand. We must be there for her when she is willing to take the chance. But we must also realize that the most dangerous time is when she is trying to leave. More women are killed then than any other time. We must continue to offer help and never give up. Most women do leave such situations eventually (DeKeseredy and Schwartz). However, the average woman tries to leave unsuccessfully 7–8 times before she finally is successful. We must be there for her when she is ready to take that step. This may not be the time. But we must not give up. We can't force her. We have asked her to make a new life. That is hard. We must provide resources and alternatives. We must invite her. But it is her decision. We must respect that.

The humanist can only set the stage, invent resources and extend an invitation. The scientific power will seek to force an outcome at any cost with no regard for the pollution created by such coercion. However, if the humanist tries to take the Other by force, the very essence of the humanistic vision is lost. To court by force is closer to rape than to love. The secrets we wished to unfold remain unfulfilled. If we must force love, then it is not love. If we must trick or swindle or in other ways try to coerce love to render its fruits, then we will never be quite satisfied with their sweetness.

Sidney Jourard expresses it nicely:

> I love her. What does this mean? . . . As she discloses her being to me or before my gaze, my existence is enriched. I am more alive. I experience myself in dimensions that she evokes, such that life is more meaningful and livable. My beloved is a mystery that I want to make transparent. But the paradox is that I cannot make my beloved do anything. I can only invite and earn the disclosure that makes her transparent. I want to know my beloved. But for me to know, she must show. And for her to show her mysteries to me, she must be assured I will respect them, take delight in them (Jourard, 1971, p. 52).

Perhaps it is because we have conceived of love as a gift and thus outside of our control that we find it so valuable. Love that can be bought or forced is only a pretense. Real love is similar to a free gift. Those seeking scientific and technological ways of controlling and predicting love will never be satisfied with their results for love will slip through their grasp. Love is not a force which we can chain to our intentions. We must all remember that at times there has been nothing that we could do to "win" a love. And at other times, we have been loved far beyond anything we could have ever predicted.

Humanistic Social Control

The conservatives want to put the Hobbesian values of obedience into place claiming we need society to protect us from each other. Rousseau, on the other hand, postulated that people were born good and corrupted by society. His solution was that we must then remake society—its social forms and its social institutions.

We must look at styles of social control. Sullivan, Tifft, and Sullivan (1997) present discipline as enthusiasm as an alternative to discipline by obedience. This strange sounding phrase means that people who are self actualized, enthused (literally, "filled with the spirit"), and have a greater purpose are trustworthy. Discipline takes care of itself. Hal Pepinsky would claim that more safety can be had with empathy and dialog than by obedience and forced conformity. In *The Geometry of Democracy and Violence,* he says democracy is responsive to the needs of others. When we communicate in dialog our perceptions and agendas shift as we take each other into account. Refusing to take the other person into account is the fundamental essence of violence.

Pepinsky and Quinney (1991) presented the idea of peacemaking criminology. Rather than wage a war on crime with more punishments, peacemaking criminology maintains that to end crime we must heal broken lives. The writer Dostoyeski wrote, "You can judge the degree of civilization of a society by visiting its prisons."

Peacemaking is more than avoiding war. Conflict resolution has taught us we need to pay attention to human needs (Burton, 1990). Unless we meet basic human needs, societies manifest all kinds of social problems. To create the peaceful society we need to create social arrangements where people flourish. We need to attend to human needs.

Maslow explores needs. Oddly enough, one might actually look at Maslow as an extended footnote to B.F. Skinner. Skinner didn't understand that people should not be a manipulatable variable. He did not understand the difference between rewards and punishments, and also failed to understand the dynamics of what are motivators for human beings.

Negative reinforcement is just not the opposite of positive reinforcement. Rewards and punishments are totally different realms. Love and meaning are rewards. Fear, imprisonment, and physical pain are examples of negative motivators. It doesn't make sense to understand love as just the opposite of imprisonment, or meaning as the reverse of physical pain. Rewards and punishments are in different theaters, each with their own different dynamics, feelings, and experiences. We are draw towards rewards. We flee away from punishments. There is a difference between pushes and pulls; the forces of attraction and repulsion are not just opposites but are different in kind.

Rewards and punishments are not on a continuum where one can be added or subtracted from the other. Removing a punishment is just not the same as a reward. One may talk about finding food or water when you are starving as a "reward." However, it is really not a "positive reinforcement" but a matter of removing a deficiency. This is a different from true positive reinforcement such as having a significant other in your life or being part of a meaningful drama. Rewards and punishments are different in kind. The pull of the positive involves a quite different dynamic than the repulsion of negative forces.

Maslow (1968) distinguishes between deficiency motivators (d-needs) and being motivators (b-needs). D-needs are the basic survival needs including food, shelter, and safety. We seek to avoid deficiencies. They operate as pushes. The B-needs are pulls. They include self esteem, meaning, and love.

Bill once took a class on "Humanism and Mysticism" with counterculture analyst Theodore Roszak. The enduring text was philosopher Henri Bergson's *The Two Sources of Religion and Morality*. The two sources are two visions of social control. The first is social obligation ("you must because you must), the second is the impetus to love. We pushed by obligation; love is an aspiration towards which we are drawn. Bergson writes in every age "exceptional souls have appeared who sensed their kinship with the soul of Everyman." (Bergson, 1935, p.95).

"It is these men who draw us toward an ideal society, while we yield to the pressure of the real one" (Bergson, 1935, p. 68). We have followed after them trying to make moral codes and recipes to enable us to repeat the peak experience. It is the perfect example of reification and institutionalization.

When things become institutionalized or reified, does that mean they automatically go wrong? It is a classic problem. We know supposed humanistic sociologists who just assume less structure is better. But that is naïve and non-sociological. We are going to have social constructions. The question is what kind? We have a friend who worries that restorative justice is going to be institutionalized. He wonders how to continue it as an ongoing open dialog even when it becomes mainstream. How do we create open social institutions with room for the human? This is a crucial question for humanistic sociology.

Humanistic Management, Humanistic Government

How do we manage people's behavior? How do we govern? When he was first elected to the Iowa legislature several years ago, a friend asked us: "What laws should I make?" We still haven't gotten back to him. Government is not just about law making. Management is not about making rules. In fact, the new rhetoric in the management literature is about managing the organizational culture.

Leadership is not about manipulating people. It is about creating a vision and a context in which people can flourish. There are two kinds of social organization: social arrangements where we are more $(1 + 1 > 2)$ and social arrangements that diminish us $(1 + 1 < 2)$. Humanistic sociology aspires to create society where people are more.

B.F. Skinner's work is an extensive body of research showing conclusively that rewards work better than punishments. For someone who studied rats and believed in determinism, it is a surprising conclusion. We must reflect on the meaning of his haunting line that "love is the use of positive reinforcement." It is probably right at least as a theory of management, government, and social control.

Positive reinforcement creates a very different world. If we use negative reinforcement, we focus on punishment and fear. The grain of truth in punishment worth keeping is feedback. Feedback is simply informational—it is just enough to let a person know they are over the line and it won't be tolerated. We must realize what force can do and what it can't do. Force can incapacitate. We must be careful that we do not overload the person so that the volume of punishment is so great that one cannot hear the message in the deafening din. If punishment is our only tool, we may quickly incapacitate people who are already wounded. We must build people up. Some cultures empower, while others produce alienation.

Ironically, humanistic social science probably owes as much to the debate with B.F. Skinner as to anything else. A mechanical metaphor would assume that people are small "widgets"—we pull the lever to make them behave in different ways. A humanistic metaphor would deal with a full human actor who is dancing on the hands of time itself. How would we create social constructions, institutions, social arrangements, social resources, and other social inventions that human actors could bring to their situations. Culture is a series of resources.

The sociological insight isn't that hard to understand:

Human behavior takes place in a context. Culture is a series of resources. The resources one has available influences how one acts. Different environments make some behaviors more likely and some less probable. By seeding resources into the environment, we can influence behavior. (Du Bois and Wright, manuscript in progress)

If culture influences how we act, then management and government is about setting the stage. What kinds of resources would be helpful to individual actors in their struggles? Humanistic social control is a different theory of management and government than manipulation, force and rules.

We cannot talk of a humanistic sociology that promotes the good without somehow accounting for evil. We need a theory of alienation. Humanistic sociology needs a Theory Of Evil. Social problems are merely symptoms of larger societal problems. Sociology shows common causes include lack of meaning, lack of empowerment, lack of community, and inability to share power. A formula for overcoming alienation includes empowerment, inventing participatory resources, meaningful roles and feeling part of a meaningful drama. We must be about creating social resources individual actors can use in their lives. This is the real meaning of the sociological imagination. As a society, we reap what we sow. Under some conditions, people flourish, while under other conditions, although the spirit is willing, people atrophy. What shall we sow?

What kind of framework do we want for organizing society or an organization? A rational roadmap might envision individuals as being ripe for manipulation. A humanistic conception of humankind pictures an organism with grand purpose and full humanity. Bill once taught at a school where they seemed to think that humanism was simply part of the phrase "godless humanism." He met writer Catherine Roberts on the train to one dissertation committee meeting. Her article "The Three Faces of Humanism" reminds that if some would say people are made in the image of God, then we should respect the sanctity of the human.

Rational planning must make room for the movement of the spirit. We must realize what rules can do and what they can't do. We must understand the difference between the letter of the law and the spirit of the law. Weber did not understand why rationality had been such a mixed blessing in organizations. Rationality does not leave room for the movement of the human.

How do we create government and organizations that respects the human? In 1959, C. Wright Mills wrote in *The Sociological Imagination* that we have learned from the Enlightenment that "increased rationality may not be assumed to make for increased freedom (1959, p. 16)."

> Science, it turns out, is not a technological Second Coming. . . . The increasing rationalization of society, the contradiction between such rationality and reason, the collapse of the assumed coincidence of reason and freedom—these developments lie back of the rise into view of the man who is 'with' rationality but without reason, who is increasingly self-rationalized and also increasingly uneasy. It is in terms of this type of man that the contemporary problem of freedom is best stated. . . .

> From the individual's standpoint, much that happens seems the result of manipulation, of management, of blind drift . . . Given these effects of the ascendant rationalization, the individual does the best he can. He gears his aspirations and his work to the situation he is in, and from which he can find no way out. In due course, he does not seek a way out: he adapts. That part of his life which is left over from work, he uses to play, to consume, 'to have fun.'. . .

Alienated from production, from work, he is also alienated from consumption, from genuine leisure (Mills, 1959, p. 168).

> In our time, what is at issue is the very nature of man, the image we have of his limits and possibilities as man. History is not yet done with its exploration of the limits and meanings of 'human nature.'. . . . Among contemporary men will there come to prevail, or even to flourish, what may be called The Cheerful Robot? . . . . there lies the simple and decisive fact that the alienated man is the antithesis of the Western image of the free man. The society in which this man, this cheerful robot, flourishes is the antithesis of the free society (p. 171).

It is the story of both science and the accompanying rational bureaucracy. B.F. Skinner in *Beyond Freedom and Dignity* boldly stated that with the move to social science, we have entered the kingdom of decisions previously reserved for the gods. As we debate issues of nuclear power, human cloning, environmental pollution and bioengineering, we make decisions about the world that a century ago would have never been dreamt. The knowledge of sociology tells us that decisions on social policy clearly shape whether people are more likely to be good or evil.

That is what the pragmatists told us a century ago. And this is the conclusion the postmodernists are re-echoing if we take them to their logical conclusion. What kind of world do we want to make? We are in the kingdom of the gods.

Skinner, of course, thought the implications of all this is that we must treat human freedom and dignity as outmoded pre-scientific concepts. Humanists would disagree and suggest instead that we must remodel our conception of science.

The question for social control is always: what kind of person do we want? It is a strange question and we often shy away from the full impact of such awesome responsibility. Yet we must make the choice or defer to someone else who does. We must design society and sociology with an eye to *what kind of human beings we want to make.* At a recent conference Lisa Bjergaard who is the Eastern Northern Dakota Director of Juvenile Corrections stated it just that boldly. In the state that has the lowest recidivism in the nation by far, she said they begin by asking what kind of person they want at the end. It is the question for all social designers.

Human Nature As a Self fulfilling Prophecy

This brings us to the question sociologists and psychologists alike have habitually tried to avoid: "what is human nature?" It is here that humanists have usually been undone by the shadow side. The politics of good and evil confront us across human history. However, we cannot avoid the question and must give at least a tentative orientation.

Human nature may not be any more than a matter of potential: not a matter of "being," but a process that is "becoming." It is a departure from "what is" to what "might be." Self is not contained, but has many faces. Human experience may vary, but we see a thread of possibilities from the best to the worse. Indeed, we recognize a familiarity in all experiences, because once we understand the

situation, we may see how we might have behaved similarly in the same situation. We can cross and connect with other lives, seeing how we might be living
those lives.

The social institutions we create will shape humans to an image. What do
we want to make? What kind of human being do we want? What is your image
of humanity?

> To opt for a theory of human ills is not only to opt for the kind of person one is
> going to have to pay deference to professionally; it is also to opt potentially for
> the kind of world one is going to wake up in, the kinds of human beings that
> one will have to come across on the street. To opt for a particular theory of hu-
> man ills is very much like falling in love in strictest sense: it is to opt for the
> presence of a certain kind of being in the world, and hence for a certain kind
> world (Becker, 1968, p. 364).

Humanistic sociology strives to bring values right through the "front door" of the
discipline and envision society in such a way as to make a better self-fulfilling
prophecy. Human nature does appear to be a self fulfilling prophecy. Some people will be good no matter how they are treated. Some people seem to screw up
irregardless of what society does. But most of us could go either way. We can
design social systems where people are likely to be good. Unfortunately, we
typically design social systems where people are more likely to resort to evil.

Fromm (1968) in an incredible article entitled "What It Means to Be Human," recommends we follow Walt Whitman in saying that "I contain multi-
tudes" and Goethe's idea that "I can conceive of no act so horrible that I cannot
imagine myself to be the author." Across so many different cultures, the human
spirit has taken so many different forms.

Some may remember third grade teacher Jane Elliot's classroom exercise in
which she divided students into brown-eyed and blue-eyed groups to teach about
prejudice and discrimination. One of the interesting side effects was that when
students were in the superior group, their scores on tests were higher; on the day
they were in the inferior group, their scores were lower; and after the exercise
everyone's scores were higher and *remained that way permanently.* As the re-
searchers said, that wasn't possible but that it appears to be what happened. The
lesson is clear: When people are treated as superior, they become superior. And
after they learned they could be superior, the lesson stuck. The self-fulfilling
prophecy exists in daily life. Perhaps like Garrison Keillor's mythical land of
Lake Woebegone, we need to create a society where everyone is above average.

Max Weber maintained sociologists should seek a verstehen approach or a
subjective understanding. Charles Cooley recommended sympathetic introspection as the method of sociology. "There but for fortune go I" might be an easy
translation of what he meant. It is a common ideology that sees how the fates of
circumstances influence who we are and our outcomes.

"I–Thou" is a different paradigm for knowledge to what we are accustomed.
Many languages actually take this concept into account and provide different
words for "you," some defining the concept of "Thou" offering respect, a closeness, a sense of sharing. English, on the other hand, forces us to use a modifier,

another inserted word of phrase, to make this distinction. Our obsession with the individual and individual values has so influenced the language that we use, the way that we think using that language, that we have difficulty in making such a sense of "Thou" as a part of our culture.

Comte had envisioned sociology as a humanitarian religion. Today, we laugh at his arrogance, but perhaps this candor was his genius. He realized that sociology is clearly in the realm of religion and forging a new shared understanding. There but for fortune go I. Is that not the sociological understanding? Our lives are entwined. Our personal problems are related to our social problems.

Comte sought to demonstrate the relationship between private problems and public issues. This is the only reason he felt that we could compel people to act together: a realization of shared fates; an enlightened self interest. This is the exact same mantle that C. Wright Mills would later take up. Reviewing what we have learned about the nature of the social bond in the first 150 years of social science, Ernest Becker wrote:

> It showed exactly what Comte had wanted: the fullest possible correlates of the dependence of personal troubles on social issues.

> The problem for all thinkers of the Enlightenment, and especially for Comte, was how to get social interest to predominate over selfish private interest. The new theory of alienation showed ethical action could not be possible where man was not supplied with self critical and socially critical knowledge, and with the possibilities of broad and responsible choices. Recurrent evils like sadism, militant hate, competitive greed, narrow-pride, calculating self-interest that takes a non-chalant view of others' lives . . . *all stem from constrictions on behavior and from shallowness of meanings;* and these could be laid in the lap of society. . . . and the kinds of choices and cognition which its institutions encourage and permit. Man could only be ethical if he was strong, and he could only be strong if he was given fullest possible cognition, and responsible control over his own powers. The only possible ethics was one which took man as a center, and which provided him with the conditions that permitted him to try to be moral.

> The antidote to evil was not to impose a crushing sense of supernatural sanction, or unthinking obligation or automatic beliefs of any kind—no matter how 'cheerful' they seem. For the first time in history it had become transparently clear that the real antidote to evil in society was to supply the possibility or depth and wholeness or experience. . . . It had never been so well understood that goodness and human nature were potentially synonymous terms; and evil was a complex reflex of the coercion of human powers (1968, pp. 325–326)

If you will note, this is also the exact solution proposed by John Dewey. And because of these beliefs he was dedicated to educating people for democracy. If you will understand his Chicago Philosophy department colleague George Herbert Mead's conception of the generalized other and his approach to social problems, you will realize that they are similar.

Postmodernism and Pragmatism

The Sociological Consciousness was probably understood *better* in the early 1900s than it is understood now. Pragmatism may have formulated it better than any other set of ideas. Our pretenses to final truths are but a detour. What kind of world would we like to make? How do we get there? And how should we travel?

The outcome of postmodernism should be to examine the consequences of different knowledge strategies. Actually this brings us back to the pragmatism of John Dewey and the whole conversation that led to the birth of the Chicago School. Pragmatism offers the way to move with and beyond both value relativity and postmodernism: What are the consequences of different knowledge strategies? The postmodernists would tell us that reality is only "make-believe." So what should we make believe?

We frankly don't understand what is advanced by postmodernism that wasn't solved by pragmatism: There is no truth. So what? There *are* consequences of different knowledge strategies. There is no real reality. So what? There *are* consequences of choosing to define the situation in different ways.

Ernest Becker wrote in his time that we live in a world of an overabundance of truth: too many truths. Perhaps this was just the clutching of a modernist man. But the remedy to his dilemma would have been Omar Khamyan's insight that to "each must come the time to decide between truth and wisdom." Wisdom would be the right truth at the right time.

In our time, postmodernists conclude properly that there is no truth. That does not mean that there is still not need for wisdom: the right insight at the right time.

The old questions of the ancient philosophers was simply: "should we find the truth or make the good?" It was decided that we should *first* find the truth and *then* we would know how to make the good. Well, sorry, the journey to find the truth didn't work out. That shouldn't be cause for eternal moaning. What it means is that we are back with the question of "how to make the good?"

Charles Lemert (1995) notes in the modernist world, the truth structured differences. Values decide what to rank from best to worst. Classes get ranked in relation to those values. In the postmodernist world, there is no truth so the ranking is more arbitrary and the power relation more obvious.

At its best, postmodernism is really a "liberation theology" and best understood when conceived of as that. But once you get free, we still have a world to make. What kind of world do we want to create? Fromm suggested clearly there are consequences to depending on how we define the situation. We can create a world where we define human nature as good and people are more likely to act like that. Ruth Benedict said in the synergistic cultures she studied, it wasn't that people never did bad things. It was that the society never gave up on them and figured someday they would come around. And they usually did.

The journey to find the truth has revealed some very interesting things. Despite the fact that what we discovered wasn't what we wanted, whatever we concluded from that journey must be the truth. What has the journey to find the truth revealed? First, that where you choose to focus determines what you see. Second, how you look determines what you see. It is almost like an old episode of *Star Trek* where each reality (or planet) defines its own time and space. So we need to decide what we want to create. If it is make believe, what should we make believe?

As important as it is, it is not enough to just deconstruct the world. We also have lives to construct. It is an arm-chair luxury to merely condemn without beginning the hard work of deciding what to recommend. We have a world to make.

Making the World

We might suggest that "I–It" knowledge has become a nuisance and a danger even to the planet. The journey of science with its abstraction of the uninvolved observer separate from the process is an abstraction that we can't afford. Pressed to its farthest frontier we have reached the end of its usefulness and it is now a danger. Science not only means possible pollution and destruction of the environment, it also means the alienation of the human.

Can Science Save Us? So far, science has always pulled us out of the fire. Maybe we would not have had the fire from which we are pulled had we not had science as it exists in modern society. Beginning social scientists believed in the myth of progress. However, we have come to learn that there are limits. We are bounded. The planet itself is encased in an atmosphere. Nuclear and environmental pollution comes back upon us. There are limits beyond which we cannot go. We would like so much to wish away any reality or limits. Pretend that there is no ozone layer that matters.

In the 1950s through the 1980s, we had to learn to live with the threat of nuclear holocaust. The explosion of the entire planet and elimination of most life forms remains a possibility. There are consequences to what we do. A science of mindless tinkering and endless curiosity eventually bumps up against them. We learn that pollution of rivers and the very air we breathe cannot go on endlessly without consequences for human life.

Fromm says that a humanistic science is based on "interest" instead of mere "curiosity." Do we care about humanity? Are we concerned with making people's lives better? Or are we just meddling?

Food supplies can be contaminated by chemical preservatives and pesticides thus poisoning us and producing, among other bad things, cancer. To put things in an ecological perspective is a whole new way of thinking. There are consequences to different actions. Species can become extinct. Water supplies can be poisoned.

Science would assume there are no limits. We can just endlessly explore. But we have learned that long before we get to the end of the journey, the scientific prodding has its limits. The ancients sought to discover the elementary building blocks of matter. They called them corpules. Today, we call them atoms. But if you will notice, the splitting of the atom not only launched us into a nuclear age, it also shattered a whole way of thinking. If the atom could be split, then there were not irreducible fundamental building blocks of matter. It became slowly abundantly clear that we were not *discovering* the truth. We were *shaping the world to an image.*

Pretending to separate the observer from the process was fool's play. The objective observer does not exist. We are tied to the planet and the process. "I" – "Thou" knowledge must be an essential part of our vision. We need a humanistic science. We must put the human back into the system.

As the deconstruction of science has reminded us, the human has always been there.

> We have found that where science has progressed the farthest, the mind has but regained from nature that which the mind has put into nature. We have found a strange footprint on the shores of the unknown. We have devised profound theories, one after another, to account for its origin. At last we have succeeded in reconstructing the creature that made the footprint. And lo! it is our own (Eddington quoted in Matson, 1964, p. 125).

This time we must put the human back into our science thorough the front door. Remember Comte's dream: a world in which politics was submitted to morals. Sociology was to gather the knowledge from which to build that consensus. This was Aristotle's dream. When he first conceived of the idea of science he imagined a science of the polis (the community). Postmodernism would claim no consensus is ever possible. Postmodernism's language keeps it safely academic and obscure. It poses no threat to the established social politics.

We are learning from our social science that there are consequences for disregarding our fellow human beings. Oddly, it is Erich Fromm (1968: 63–64), a psychologist, who has the crucial sociological understanding: *you can treat people almost any way, but you can't do it without consequences.* Children growing up absurd in an alienating environment take guns to school and kill their classmates. Nations that have higher income disparities between the rich and poor have higher crime rates.

Ironically, the Christian Right is correct about the separation of church and state. We can't really separate values from social policy. Now, we just need to debate *which* values. The Founding Fathers thought such an objective separation of values and action was possible only because in the background *they believed in science.* They thought science could be used to shape a shared understanding to make the world.

Sociologists and other social scientists know some lessons. As Becker iterated we can actually sketch some conclusions. Human beings need love and human contact. Without it infants die or at very least do not grow and thrive. The human organism needs meaning. People need to feel empowered. If we do not create societies that address human needs, we create alienation.

Humanistic sociology is really an ongoing merging of religious and philosophical insights. All religions have a value similar to the golden rule. Perhaps, this is why August Comte had originally conceived of sociology as a humanitarian religion. It was to be a shared understanding of our commitment to each other.

We must move beyond behaviorism and deterministic science. Carl Jung noted that "the mind lives by aims as well as causes" (Matson, 1964, p. 208). This is reminiscent of the early sociologists quest to find the elementary social forces. If you will recall, the elementary social forces are human purposes. In the late 1800s, sociologists were trying to agree on a complete definitive list of human needs. When they couldn't get a list that looked like a periodic atomic table of the elements, they abandoned the conversation. We do not need to agree on the exact naming and delineation of human needs. We have always been struck by the fact that all lists of basic human needs look very similar. The precise naming or categories differs from theorist to theorist. Who cares what we call them? Your list may not look like ours but all categorization schemes really sketch much of the same territory. We don't need an exact atomic chart of needs as the early sociologists supposed. We don't need such analytical dissection. It is enough to acknowledge that human needs are critical. Social systems must address them.

Values—Which Values?

If humanistic sociology is to make values matter in designing the world, we must ask: which values? The sociologist should not strive to be without values. Cultural relativity means taking your values off long enough to see. It does not mean to be without values. Objectivity means putting things in perspective. It really means honesty—not to falsify things. The core element of objectivity is "respect." Respect according to Erich Fromm is from the original root meaning "to look at." We certainly need to be streetwise in our knowledge and non-naive in our humanism. We must bring our values to work. Humanism is not a hobby we do after work: making a better world must be the real work of sociology.

Relativism is grounded if we can obtain one referent. That reference point is human welfare. What is good for the person? Once we ground humanistic science in that understanding, everything changes. This is not a new idea. This was Comte's notion, Ward's, Small's, Lynd's, Fromm's, Maslow's, and Becker's. *Humanistic sociology embraces the value that we must relate everything to what is good for people.* This is what has been meant from the beginning as the idea of a humanistic sociology.

As Becker noted (1971, p. 152): "the brilliant work of Erich Fromm is the best synthesis . . . to emerge in our epoch, and it is this we shall have to build." It is still true today. In *Revolution of Hope,* Fromm proposed the very same standard Robert Lynd had recommended thirty years earlier: we can overcome the relativism of science if we agree upon one value—the promotion of human welfare: "Humanistic ethics . . . is formally based on the principle that only man himself can determine the criteria for virtue. 'Good' is what is good for man and 'evil' is what is detrimental to man: the sole criterion of ethical value being man's welfare." (Fromm, 1947: 22)

Fromm (1968 p. 96) suggested we obtain an humanistic "science" if we begin with the value "that it is desirable that a living system should grow and produce the maximum of virtue and intrinsic harmony." (1947, p. 163).

Ernest Becker (1968: 327-346) said when it first occurred to him that self esteem is the value for synthesizing the social sciences, he thought it must be too simple. But that is precisely what it is. *Self esteem—a subjective feeling of well being—should be the referent value for a science of humanity. Social institutions should answer human needs.*

We would also recommend Ruth Benedict's concept of synergy. Ironically a young new Ph.D. by the name of Abraham Maslow went to work for her shortly after graduation. He was so fascinated by the energy of her personality that he made a career out of identifying and studying people he felt were models of a healthy personality. Ruth Benedict was in fact Maslow's first model of the self actualized person. She herself was interested in the interrelationship between personality and culture, and imagined an ideal society based on synergy. In *The Farthest Reaches of Human Nature*, he began to explore Benedict's idea of a synergistic culture that promoted the conditions for a better life. Synergy thus got smuggled into psychology through the back door as it were and sociology has still not gotten around to exploring the implications of Benedict's argument. The self-actualization of a humanistic psychology is incomplete without a companion sociology that focuses upon synergy (Du Bois, 2001).

In actuality, Benedict had discovered the first synthesis that emerges once we leave behind a value-free science and move firmly into the direction of an integrated science in the service of human needs. As Bill argued in his dissertation on humanistic sociology, Ruth Benedict solved two philosophical problems which had been outstanding for more than two thousand years. Synergy provides an operational definition of "the Good" and also an operational definition of "Love."

Synergy is win-win arrangements between the individual good and the communal good, the person and the organization, and between individuals. Anything less, is impractical. Losers always create unwanted negative consequences. Alienation does not work.

> From all comparative material the conclusion that emerges is that societies where non-aggression is conspicuous have social orders in which the individual by the same act and at the same time serves his own advantage and that of the group. The problem is one of social engineering and depends upon how large the areas of mutual advantage are in any society. Non-aggression occurs not because people are unselfish and pursue social obligations above personal desire, but when social arrangements makes these two identical (Maslow, 1971, p. 40).

As Benedict (1970, p. 55) notes, "the fundamental condition of peace is federation for mutual advantage." To create a successful society, we must create a win-win situation for everyone and every entity involved.

Where do values fit in sociology? The central question is whether values belong as the mainstream focus for the work of sociologists or whether they should be after work avocations and hobbies. As *American Sociologist* editor Larry Nichols pointed out Ogburn who sought scientific respectability for sociology and was so critical of an ameliorative social science, consulted with the federal government on issues of social planning in the 1930s. Talcott Parsons who often became the straw man for C. Wright Mills' writings, "wrote against fascism, resisted McCarthyism, and wrote about the reform of education in the U.S." Sociologists have always cared about social problems. Indeed that is why we have all entered the field. The question is one of methods. Where do values fit?

Although William Foote Whyte is not normally claimed as a humanistic sociologist, a recent Sociological Practice Association annual meeting in honor of him was appropriately entitled "Using Sociology for Good." Whyte's idea of action research is appropriate for humanistic sociology. Effort is brought to bear upon an organization or problem in an attempt to change it and make it better.

Comte envisioned a society where we could better live the dream. Truly credible scholarship keeps the human possibility alive and furthers its direction. We also must take sociology into the world and change it. To record "what is" is not enough. We must report that "what is" suggests alternatives and possibilities that could be followed. We must invent new social resources and alternatives. Sociology is precisely in the business of re-visioning society. If society is theater, then how do we stage the dream? It is an old quest. Starry-eyed youths enter the field eager for the romance of changing the world. As we grow to maturity, we put aside the grandeur and begin the day-to-day task of living. But some of the old dream never quite goes away. As people retire, we find them once again challenging youth with the same old hope. We cannot hold out the promise of sociology just at the beginning and the end of careers. The real mid-life crisis that nags us in our sleep and comes bursting through as we turn back to the world from peak experience is: how do we return the old question to the mainstream of the field? What does it mean to be a humanist and what are the implications for sociology? How do we build upon meaning, values, and the quest for a better world and make it the work of sociology?

Conclusion

We need some referent if we are to escape from relativism. What should be our evaluative standard? Humanism simply means people have human needs and social systems should address them. It also embraces incorporating the sphere of values that Jean Kilbourne (1979) would suggest we have labeled feminine and neglected. Love and concern for human welfare would be first. It is about social amelioration.

We would recommend two evaluative standards: (1) Human Needs: Humanistic sociology begins with the proposition that social systems should meet human needs. Maslow and humanistic psychology laid the foundation for a humanistic social science by exploring basic human needs. The whole conversation of humanistic sociology is about how. We need to empower and invent resources. (2) Synergy: The second evaluative criteria for social inventions should be synergy. We should fashion win-win arrangements between individuals, between the organization and the person, and between the communal good and the individual good.

Humanistic sociology begins with the critique of value free science and embraces the counterculture's effort to create alternative social forms. Science is not going to discover a truth that will tell us how to live. We must choose our values. Following Nietzsche's "Will to Power," humanistic psychology recognized that all knowledge claims are about shaping humanity in an image. Human nature is a self fulfilling prophecy. We need a society that offers meaningful roles and the depth of experience. A humanistic society creates a context in which people flourish.

Humanistic sociology begins with a recognition of our common humanity. It values "I–Thou" knowledge rather than an "I–It" knowledge that treats people and the environment only as objects for manipulation. Humanistic social control emphasizes rewards and positive motivators rather than the authoritarian social control of obedience. A humanistic sociology respects the human. If we value the human, we must allow people free will which means indeterminacy enters the picture. A deterministic science ultimately mean elimination of the human. A humanistic sociology realizes that "there but for fortune go I." It makes social institutions with that in mind.

Humanistic sociology must be forever breaking the mold. It must be breaking out of the institutionalized "me," to use Mead's terms, and returning to the dialog and open creativity of the "I." Humanism must strive to create social forms and social institutions which bring more of the human spirit into play. This creation must also be true for our professional organizations.

Alfred McClung Lee founded the Society for the Study of Social Problems (SSSP). When it became too large and institutionalized, he went on to found the Association for Humanist Sociology (AHS). The Clinical Sociology Association (now Sociological Practice Association—SPA) and the Society for Applied Sociology (SAS) were also founded as efforts to return sociology to the vision of early sociologists in which sociology was about making the good.

We have no idea whether any of these organizations will be vital forces for social change in the future or just survive as esoteric clubs for academicians. What we do know is at its core sociology, the larger discipline, must return to its roots and re-embrace the vision that gave it birth. Sociology must once again become the study of how to make a better world.

Notes

1. An earlier version was the lead article in *The American Sociologist*, Special Issue on Humanistic Sociology, Volume 33, No. 4, 2002, pp. 5–36.

Bibliography

Addams, Jane. *Democracy and Social Ethics.* Introduction by Charlene Haddock Seigfried. Chicago: University of Illinois Press, 2002 (original 1902).

Arcaro, Tom and Chrissy Kilgariff. "Humanistic Sociology and Darwin: An Argument for a Sociobiological Approach." paper presented at *Association for Humanist Sociology* Meeting, Madison, WI, October 2002, http://www.elon.edu/arcaro/titles/partiv.htm.

Bardwick, Judith. *In Transition: How Feminism, Sexual Liberation and the Search for Self-Fulfillment Have Altered Our Lives.* Holt, Rinehart, and Winston, 1979.

Becker, Ernest. *The Structure of Evil: An Essay on the Unification of the Science of Man.* New York: Free Press, 1968.

———. *The Lost Science of Man.* New York: G. Braziller, 1971.

———. *Escape From Evil: An Essay on the Unification of the Science of Man.* New York: Free Press, 1975.

———. "Toward the merger of animal and human studies." *Philosophy of the Social Sciences* 4: 235–254, 1974.

Bell, Wendell. *Foundations of Futures Studies: Volume 2: Values, Objectivity, and the Good Society. Science for a New Era.* New Brunswick, NJ: Transaction Publishers, 1997.

Benedict, Ruth. "The Good Culture," *The American Anthropologist.* New York: Houghton Mifflin Company, 1970.

———. "Synergy: Patterns of the Good Culture," *The American Anthropologist.* Volume 72 , No. 2, 1970.

Bergson, Henri. *The Two Sources of Morality and Religion.* Translated by R. Ashley, Audvra and Claudesley Brereton with assistance of W. Horsfall Carter. Garden City, New York: Doubleday, 1935.

Bork, Robert H., *Slouching towards Gomorrah: Modern Liberalism and American Decline,* New York: ReganBooks, c1996.

Boulding, Kenneth. Keynote address delivered to Southwest Sociological Association, Dallas, 1977.

———. *Human Betterment.* Beverly Hills, CA: Sage, 1985.

Buber, Martin. *Between Man and Man.* Boston: Beacon Press, 1955.

———. *I and Thou.* Translated by Walter Kaufmann. New York: Scribner, 1970.

Burton, John. *Conflict: Resolution and Provention.* New York: St. Martin's Press, 1990.

Carey, Mark in Darrol Bussler, Mark Carey, and William Du Bois, "Coming Full Circle: A County-Community Restorative Justice Partnership." in William Du Bois and R. Dean Wright, *Applying Sociology: Making a Better World.* Boston: Allyn and Bacon, 2001.

Chugerman, Samuel. (1939). *Lester F. Ward: The American Aristotle.* New York: Octagon Books, 1965.

Clark, Ramsey. *Crime in America.* New York: Simon & Schuster, 1970.

Cronk, George. "George Herbert Mead." *The Internet Encyclopedia of Philosophy*, http://www.utm.edu/research/iep/m/mead.htm#The%20Nature%20of%20History.

Daly, Martin and Wilson, Margo. *The Truth about Cinderella: A Darwinian View of Paternal Love.* New Haven and London: Yale University Press (1998).

Dawkins, Richard. *The Selfish Gene.* New York: Oxford University Press (1976).

Deagan, Mary Jo. *Jane Addams and the Men of the Chicago School.* New Brunswick, NJ: Transaction Publishers, 1988.

DeKeseredy, Walter S. and Martin D. Schwartz, *Contemporary Criminology,* Wadsworth, 1996, p. 322.

Dennett, Daniel. *Darwin's Dangerous Idea.* New York: Touchstone, 1995.

Du Bois, William. "Love, Synergy, and the Magical: The Foundations of a Humanistic Sociology." Dissertation, Oklahoma State University, 1983.
"A Framework for Doing Applied Sociology," in William Du Bois and R. Dean Wright, *Applying Sociology: Making a Better World.* Boston: Allyn and Bacon, 2001.

Du Bois, William and R. Dean Wright, *Applying Sociology: Making a Better World.* Boston: Allyn and Bacon, 2001.

———. "What Is Humanistic Sociology?" *The American Sociologist,* Volume 33, No. 4, 2002.

Edgerton, Robert B. *Sick Societies: Challenging the Myth of Primitive Harmony.* New York: The Free Press, 1992.

Frankl, S. *Will to Meaning.* New York: New American Library, 1965.

Fromm, Erich. *The Art of Loving.* New York: Harper and Row, 1956.

———. *Man for Himself.* New York: Fawcett Premier Books, 1947.

———. *The Revolution of Hope.* New York: Harper and Row, 1968.

———. *The Sane Society.* New York: Rinehart , 1955.

———. *Escape from Freedom,* New York: Henry Holt and Company, 1941.

Glass, John F., and John R. Staude. *Humanistic Society: Today's Challenge to Sociology.* Pacific Palisades: Goodyear Publishing, 1972.

Gouldner, Alvin W. *The Coming Crisis of Western Sociology.* New York: Basic Books, 1970.

Griffin, Susan. *Woman and Nature: The Roaring Inside Her.* New York: Harper and Row, 1978.

Hampden-Turner, Charles. *Radical Man.* Cambridge: Schenkman Publishing, 1970.

Harris, "Ruth Benedict and Her Lost Manuscript." *Psychology Today* , 1970.

Hocking, William Ernest. *Types of Philosophy.* New York: Scribner, 1959.

Horney, Karen. *The Neurotic Personality of Our Time.* New York: W.W. Norton and Co., Inc., 1937.

Horowitz, Irving Louis. *The New Sociology.* New York: Oxford University Press, 1964

Hume, David. *An Enquiry Concerning the Principles of Morals.* Edited by J. B. Schneewind. Indianapolis: Hackett Publishing Company, 1983 (c. 1751).

Jampolsky, Gerald G. *Love is Letting Go of Fear.* New York: Bantam Books, 1979.

Jourard, Sidney M. *Disclosing Man to Himself.* Princeton: Van Nostrand, 1968.
———. *Healthy Personality: An Approach from the Viewpoint of Humanistic Psychology.* New York: Macmillan, 1974.
Personal Adjustment: An Approach Through The Study Of Healthy Personality. New York, Macmillan, 1958.
———. *The Transparent Self.* Princeton: VanNostrand Reinhold, 1971.
Jung, Carl G. *Man and His Symbols.* London: Aldus Books, 1964.
Kanter, Rosabeth Moss. *Men and Women of the Corporation.* New York: Basic Books, 1977.
Kilbourne, Jean, Joseph Vitagliano, and Patricia Stallone. *Killing Us Softly: Advertising's Image Of Women.* Film by Jean Kilbourne. Cambridge, Mass.: Cambridge Documentary Films, c1979.
Lee, Alfred McClung. *Toward Humanist Sociology.* Englewood Cliffs: Prentice-Hall, 1973.
———. *Knowledge for Whom?* New York: Oxford University Press, 1978.
Lemert, Charles. *Sociology After the Crisis.* Boulder, CO: Westview Press, 1995.
Lieberman, Trudy. *Slanting the Story: The Forces that Shape the News.* New York: The New Press, 2000.
Lipset, Seymour Martin And Sheldon S. Wolin, Editors. *The Berkeley Student Revolt: Facts And Interpretations.* Garden City, NY, Anchor Books, 1965.
Luhrmann, T. M. *Of Two Minds.* New York: Alfred Knopf, 2000.
Lynd, Robert S. *Knowledge for What?* Princeton: Princeton University Press, 1939.
Maslow, Abraham. *The Psychology of Science: A Reconnaissance.* New York: Harper and Row, 1966.
———. *Toward a Psychology of Being.* New York: Van Nostrand, 1968.
———. *The Farthest Reaches of Human Nature.* New York: Viking Press, 1971.
Matson, Floyd W. *The Broken Image; Man, Science And Society.* New York, G. Braziller: 1964.
May, Rollo. *Love and Will.* New York: W.W. Norton and Company, 1969.
The Courage to Create. New York: W.W. Norton and Company, 1975.
McLuhan, Marshall. *Understanding Media.* New York: McGraw, 1964.
Mead, George Herbert. *Mind, Self and Society.* Charles W. Morris, Ed. Chicago: University of Chicago Press, 1967.
———. *The Philosophy of the Act* , ed. C. W. Morris *et al.* Chicago: University of Chicago Press, 1938.
Mead, Margaret. *Ruth Benedict.* New York: Columbia University Press, 1974.
Merchant, Carolyn. *The Death of Nature: Women, Ecology, and the Scientific Revolution.* New York: Harper and Row, 1980.
Miller, A. *For Your Own Good: Hidden Cruelty in Child-Rearing and the Roots of Violence.* New York: Noonday Press, 1990 [1983].
Mills, C. Wright. *The Sociological Imagination.* New York: Oxford University Press, 1959.
Nesbit, Robert A. "Sociology as an Art Form." *Pacific Sociological Review*, 5, no. 2 (Fall 1962): 67–74.
Nietzsche, Friedrich Wilhelm. *The Will to Power.* Translated by Walter Kaufmann and R. J. Hollingsdale. New York: Vintage Books, 1968.

Nyden, Philip, Anne Figert, Mark Shibley, and Darryl Burrows (eds). *Building Community: Social Science in Action.* Thousand Oaks, CA: Pine Forge Press, 1997.

Ortega y Gasset, Jose. (1941). *History as a System.* New York: Norton, 1961.

Pepinsky, Hal and Richard Quinney. *Criminology As Peacemaking.* Bloomington, Ind.: Indiana University Press, 1991.

Pepinsky, Hal. *The Geometry Of Violence And Democracy.* Bloomington, Ind.: Indiana University Press, 1991.

———. "Safety from Personal Violence: Empathy and Listening." in William Du Bois and R. Dean Wright, *Applying Sociology: Making a Better World.* Boston: Allyn and Bacon, 2001.

Pepinsky, H.E. (1991). *The Geometry of Violence And Democracy.* Bloomington, IN.: Indiana University Press.

Pinker, Steven. *The Blank Slate: The Modern Denial of Human Nature.* New York: Viking, 2002

Roberts, Catherine. "The Three Faces of Humanism." *Sunrise* (February 1981), pp. 177–182 and (March 1981), pp. 208–215.

Rogers, Carl R. *On Becoming a Person.* Boston: Houghton Mifflin Company, 1961.

———. *On Personal Power.* New York: Dell Publishing, 1977.

Roszak Theodore. *The Makings of Counterculture: Technological Society and Its Youthful Opposition.* Garden City: Doubleday & Company, 1969.

———. *The Unfinished Animal.* New York: Harper and Row, 1975.

———. *Person / Plant: The Creative Disintegration of Industrial Society.* New York: Anchor Press, 1979.

———. Presentation. The Sonoma Institute, Bodega, California, 1980

Scimecca, Joseph. *Society And Freedom : An Introduction To Humanist Sociology.* 2nd ed. Chicago: Nelson-Hall, c1995.

Simmel, Georg. *The Sociology of Georg Simmel.* Translated by Kurt H. Wolff. Glencoe, Ill.: The Free Press, 1950.

Singer, Peter. *A Darwinian Left: Politics, Evolution, and Cooperation.* New Haven and London: Yale University Press (1999).

Skinner, B. F. *Beyond Freedom and Dignity.* New York: Knopf, 1971.

Sorokin, Pitirim. *The Reconstruction of Humanity.* Boston: Beacon Press, 1948.

———. *Altruistic Love: A Study of American "Good Neighbors" and Christian Saints.* Boston: Beacon Press, 1950.

———. *Explorations in Altruistic Love and Behavior: A Symposium.* Boston: Beacon Press, 1950.

———. *The Ways and Power of Love.* Boston: Beacon Press, 1951.

Forms and Techniques of Altruistic and Spiritual Growth: A Symposium. Boston: Beacon Press, 1954.

Sullivan, Dennis, Larry Tifft, and John Sullivan. "Discipline as Enthusiasm," paper presented *Association for Humanist Sociology* Meetings, Pittsburgh, 1997.

Tillich Paul. *Love, Power, and Justice.* London: Oxford University Press, 1954.

Ward, Lester F. *Glimpses of the Cosmos.* 6 Volumes. 1918.

Warmoth, Arthur. Personal Conversations.

Weber, Max. "Science as a Vocation." and "Politics as a Vocation." Originally
    speeches at Munich University, 1918, published in 1919 by Duncker &
    Humblodt, Munich.
Yankelovich, Daniel. *Coming to Public Judgment: Making Democracy Work in
    a Complex World.* Syracuse University Press, 1991.

About the Authors

William Du Bois and R. Dean Wright are the editors of *Applying Sociology: Making a Better World* and have collaborated on a number of articles.

William Du Bois is the author of *Getting the World You Want*. He is a leader in humanistic sociology and applied sociology and has written widely on prevention and the good society. He received his Ph.D. in sociology from Oklahoma State and wrote his dissertation on Love and the Good Society while in residence in one of the two humanistic psychology departments in the country at Sonoma State University. He has consulted with a wide variety of organizations ranging from women's crisis centers and juvenile group homes to businesses and state government. As CEO of a chamber of commerce, his work transformed an Iowa community reeling from the first major bank closing at the start of the 1980's farm crisis. Students voted him "Teacher of the Year" at South Dakota University in 2001 and he is currently at Southwest Minnesota State University.

R. Dean Wright is the Ellis and Nelle Levitt Distinguished Professor Emeritus of Sociology at Drake University, Des Moines. He has published four books and over 100 professional articles. Wright has chaired the Governor's Task Force on Homelessness, the state Juvenile and Criminal Justice Council, the Des Moines Salvation Army and the Des Moines Area Religious Council. He has given numerous awards for outstanding community service from Drake University and the Des Moines community, received the Iowa Corrections Association Public Service Award, the Midwest Sociological Society Award for Distinguished Service and been inducted into the Iowa Volunteer Hall of Fame. He served as Grand Marshal for graduation at Drake University for over ten years. Over his career, he has also continued the work he did as a Fulbright Scholar on the Anglo-Indian Community of India. Professor Wright's wife, Susan, is also a professor of sociology at Drake and he and she have each been president of the Midwest Sociological Society. His son is completing his Ph.D. in Sociology and his daughter-in-law has a M.A. and works as an applied sociologist.